ETHICS
OF THE FATHERS
פִּרְקֵי אָבוֹת

Translated and Annotated
with an Introduction

by

PHILIP BIRNBAUM

✳

HEBREW PUBLISHING COMPANY
79 DELANCEY STREET, NEW YORK

III

סֵדֶר בְּמִסְדָּרָה שֶׁל
הִיבְּרוּ פּוּבְּלִישִׁינְג קוֹמְפַּנִי, נְיוּ־יוֹרְק

Typography by Hebrew Publishing Co., New York
Printed and bound in the United States of America,
by Montauk Book Mfg. Co., Inc., New York

FOREWORD

The purpose of this completely new translation of *Pirke Avoth* is to render the contents of our priceless literary gem easily intelligible to men and women of today. This edition is designed primarily for the use of teachers and students. Each wise maxim and ethical principle, tersely expressed in *Pirke Avoth*, should serve as excellent source material for classroom discussion of the spiritual aspects of Israel and the classic style of the Mishnah.

Every effort has been focused on making the new translation readily understood. Wherever necessary, an interpretive phrase has been inserted within square brackets so that the reader may apprehend the thought immediately. The running commentary, containing biographical sketches and various points of interest, has been made as compactly brief as possible. Since brevity is the soul of wit, the writer has anxiously avoided rambling discourses. The authors of the Mishnah were men of few words, and it is for us to emulate their exquisite style as exemplified in the *Ethics of the Fathers*.

The following parallel columns will illustrate the difference between the old English translation and the new. The extracts for comparison are taken from the first chapter of *Avoth*.

THE NEW TRANSLATION	THE OLD TRANSLATION
The world is based upon three principles: Torah, worship, and kindliness.	Upon three things the world is based: upon the Torah, upon the Temple service, and upon the practice of charity.
Let your house be wide open; treat the poor as members of your own family.	Let thy house be open wide; let the poor be the members of thy household.
When the parties in a lawsuit are standing before you, regard them both as guilty; but when they go away from you, after having submitted to the judgment, regard them both as innocent.	When the parties to a suit are standing before thee, let them both be regarded by thee as guilty, but when they are departed from thy presence, regard them both as innocent, the verdict having been acquiesced in by them.

FOREWORD

Where a given verse is quoted for homiletical purposes, the entire passage would lack coherence should that verse be translated literally. For instance, the phrase למען צדקו (Isaiah 42:21) literally refers to God's righteousness, but in a Mishnah passage it is taken as an allusion to the potential righteousness of Israel. Hence, the biblical verse cited by Rabbi Ḥananya ben Akashya has been translated here: "The Lord was pleased, for the sake of [Israel's] righteousness, to render the Torah great and glorious."

This plainly readable translation, intended for students who no longer speak the English of King James's day, is free from archaic forms. The Hebrew text is carefully vocalized, and divided into sentences and clauses by the use of modern punctuation marks. The type which was cast expressly for *Ha-Siddur Ha-Shalem*, including *Pirke Avoth*, combines clearness with compactness and is restful to the eye. Every modern technical facility has been employed in the preparation of this edition. The writer sincerely trusts that all students of this book will succeed in gaining a clearer appreciation of the *Ethics of the Fathers*.

It is hoped that a better and more widely disseminated understanding of our religious resources will result from this edition. It remains only to emphasize that such an inspiring book as *Pirke Avoth* does not become the real possession of a person unless its contents are impressed upon his mind and influence his everyday life.

PHILIP BIRNBAUM

May, 1949.

האי מאן דבעי למהוי חסידא, לקיים מילי דאבות (בבא קמא ל׳, א).

He who desires to be virtuous must fulfill the precepts of *Avoth.*

פִּרְקֵי אָבוֹת

Recited on the Sabbaths between *Pesaḥ* and *Rosh Hashanah*

כָּל יִשְׂרָאֵל יֵשׁ לָהֶם חֵלֶק לָעוֹלָם הַבָּא, שֶׁנֶּאֱמַר: וְעַמֵּךְ כֻּלָּם צַדִּיקִים, לְעוֹלָם יִירְשׁוּ אָרֶץ; נֵצֶר מַטָּעַי, מַעֲשֵׂה יָדַי לְהִתְפָּאֵר.

פֶּרֶק רִאשׁוֹן

א. מֹשֶׁה קִבֵּל תּוֹרָה מִסִּינַי, וּמְסָרָהּ לִיהוֹשֻׁעַ, וִיהוֹשֻׁעַ לִזְקֵנִים, וּזְקֵנִים לִנְבִיאִים, וּנְבִיאִים מְסָרוּהָ לְאַנְשֵׁי כְנֶסֶת הַגְּדוֹלָה. הֵם אָמְרוּ שְׁלֹשָׁה דְבָרִים: הֱווּ מְתוּנִים בַּדִּין, וְהַעֲמִידוּ תַלְמִידִים הַרְבֵּה, וַעֲשׂוּ סְיָג לַתּוֹרָה.

ב. שִׁמְעוֹן הַצַּדִּיק הָיָה מִשְּׁיָרֵי כְנֶסֶת הַגְּדוֹלָה. הוּא הָיָה אוֹמֵר: עַל שְׁלֹשָׁה דְבָרִים הָעוֹלָם עוֹמֵד: עַל הַתּוֹרָה, וְעַל הָעֲבוֹדָה, וְעַל גְּמִילוּת חֲסָדִים.

ג. אַנְטִיגְנוֹס אִישׁ סוֹכוֹ קִבֵּל מִשִּׁמְעוֹן הַצַּדִּיק. הוּא הָיָה אוֹמֵר: אַל תִּהְיוּ כַּעֲבָדִים הַמְשַׁמְּשִׁים אֶת הָרַב עַל מְנָת לְקַבֵּל פְּרָס, אֶלָּא הֱווּ כַּעֲבָדִים הַמְשַׁמְּשִׁים אֶת הָרַב שֶׁלֹּא עַל מְנָת לְקַבֵּל פְּרָס, וִיהִי מוֹרָא שָׁמַיִם עֲלֵיכֶם.

אבות, one of the sixty-three tractates of the Mishnah, deals with the ethical principles given by the fathers of Jewish tradition who flourished over a period of nearly five centuries, from the time of the last prophet to the end of the second century. Having achieved a place in the Prayerbook, *Avoth* became the most popular of all the books of the Mishnah and its contents exercised a most salutary influence on the Jewish people. The custom of reading *Pirke Avoth* ("Chapters of the Fathers") on Sabbath afternoons was originally limited, it seems, to the period between *Pesaḥ* and *Shavuoth*. A sixth chapter, derived from a source other than the Mishnah, was added to the five chapters of *Avoth* in order to provide a separate chapter for each of the six Sabbaths between the two festivals. The sixth chapter, called *Kinyan*

ETHICS OF THE FATHERS

Recited on the Sabbaths between Pesaḥ and Rosh Hashanah

All Israel have a share in the world to come, as it is said: "Your people shall all be righteous; they shall possess the land forever; they are a plant of my own, the work of my hands, wherein I may glory."[1]

CHAPTER ONE

1. Moses received the Torah at Sinai and handed it down to Joshua; Joshua to the elders; the elders to the prophets; and the prophets handed it down to the men of the Great Assembly. The latter said three things: Be patient in the administration of justice; develop many students; and make a fence for the Torah.

2. Simeon the Just was one of the last survivors of the Great Assembly. He used to say: The world is based on three principles: Torah, worship, and kindliness.

3. Antigonus of Sokho received the oral tradition from Simeon the Just. He used to say: Be not like servants who serve the master for the sake of receiving a reward, but be like servants who serve the master without the expectation of receiving a reward; and let the fear of Heaven be upon you.

Torah ("The Acquisition of Torah"), was chosen to be read on the Sabbath preceding *Shavuoth*, the anniversary of the giving of the Torah, because its subject-matter is almost exclusively in praise of the Torah. The liturgical use of *Avoth* on Sabbath afternoons is mentioned in the *Siddur* of Amram Gaon (ninth century).

כל ישראל introduces each chapter of *Avoth* in the Prayerbook. It is an excerpt from Mishnah Sanhedrin 11:1.

תורה consists of two parts: the written law and the oral law. The written law is contained in the Five Books of Moses, and the oral law consists of the traditional interpretations and amplifications handed down by word of mouth from generation to generation until finally embodied in the talmudic literature.

כנסת הגדולה a legislative body of 120 men said to have functioned during and after the Persian period in Jewish history, about 500-300 before the common era.

סיג לתורה additional regulations, designed to preserve the biblical laws.

אנטיגנוס means to say that virtue must not be contingent upon any hope of external appreciation. מורא שמים reverence for God.

[1] *Isaiah* 60:21.

2

ד. יוֹסֵי בֶּן יוֹעֶזֶר, אִישׁ צְרֵדָה, וְיוֹסֵי בֶּן יוֹחָנָן, אִישׁ
יְרוּשָׁלַיִם, קִבְּלוּ מֵהֶם. יוֹסֵי בֶּן יוֹעֶזֶר, אִישׁ צְרֵדָה, אוֹמֵר: יְהִי
בֵיתְךָ בֵית וָעַד לַחֲכָמִים, וֶהֱוֵי מִתְאַבֵּק בַּעֲפַר רַגְלֵיהֶם, וֶהֱוֵי
שׁוֹתֶה בַצָּמָא אֶת דִּבְרֵיהֶם.

ה. יוֹסֵי בֶּן יוֹחָנָן, אִישׁ יְרוּשָׁלַיִם, אוֹמֵר: יְהִי בֵיתְךָ פָּתוּחַ
לָרְוָחָה, וְיִהְיוּ עֲנִיִּים בְּנֵי בֵיתֶךָ, וְאַל תַּרְבֶּה שִׂיחָה עִם הָאִשָּׁה.
בְּאִשְׁתּוֹ אָמְרוּ, קַל וָחֹמֶר בְּאֵשֶׁת חֲבֵרוֹ. מִכָּאן אָמְרוּ חֲכָמִים:
כָּל הַמַּרְבֶּה שִׂיחָה עִם הָאִשָּׁה גּוֹרֵם רָעָה לְעַצְמוֹ, וּבוֹטֵל
מִדִּבְרֵי תוֹרָה, וְסוֹפוֹ יוֹרֵשׁ גֵּיהִנֹּם.

ו. יְהוֹשֻׁעַ בֶּן פְּרַחְיָה וְנִתַּי הָאַרְבֵּלִי קִבְּלוּ מֵהֶם. יְהוֹשֻׁעַ בֶּן
פְּרַחְיָה אוֹמֵר: עֲשֵׂה לְךָ רַב, וּקְנֵה לְךָ חָבֵר, וֶהֱוֵי דָן אֶת כָּל
הָאָדָם לְכַף זְכוּת.

ז. נִתַּי הָאַרְבֵּלִי אוֹמֵר: הַרְחֵק מִשָּׁכֵן רָע, וְאַל תִּתְחַבֵּר
לָרָשָׁע, וְאַל תִּתְיָאֵשׁ מִן הַפֻּרְעָנוּת.

ח. יְהוּדָה בֶּן טַבַּי וְשִׁמְעוֹן בֶּן שָׁטַח קִבְּלוּ מֵהֶם. יְהוּדָה בֶּן
טַבַּי אוֹמֵר: אַל תַּעַשׂ עַצְמְךָ כְּעוֹרְכֵי הַדַּיָּנִים, וּכְשֶׁיִּהְיוּ בַּעֲלֵי
הַדִּין עוֹמְדִים לְפָנֶיךָ, יִהְיוּ בְעֵינֶיךָ כִּרְשָׁעִים, וּכְשֶׁנִּפְטָרִים
מִלְּפָנֶיךָ, יִהְיוּ בְעֵינֶיךָ כְּזַכָּאִים, כְּשֶׁקִּבְּלוּ עֲלֵיהֶם אֶת הַדִּין.

ט. שִׁמְעוֹן בֶּן שָׁטַח אוֹמֵר: הֱוֵי מַרְבֶּה לַחֲקֹר אֶת הָעֵדִים,
וֶהֱוֵי זָהִיר בִּדְבָרֶיךָ, שֶׁמָּא מִתּוֹכָם יִלְמְדוּ לְשַׁקֵּר.

י. שְׁמַעְיָה וְאַבְטַלְיוֹן קִבְּלוּ מֵהֶם. שְׁמַעְיָה אוֹמֵר: אֱהַב אֶת
הַמְּלָאכָה, וּשְׂנָא אֶת הָרַבָּנוּת, וְאַל תִּתְוַדַּע לָרָשׁוּת.

יוסי . . . ויוסי In this and the following four paragraphs are given the names
of the five *Zugoth*, "pairs" of leading scholars, who were president and vice-
president of the Sanhedrin in the course of 150 years, the period preceding
the *Tannaim*.

4. Yosé ben Yo'ezer of Zeredah and Yosé ben Yoḥanan of Jerusalem, received the oral tradition from the preceding. Yosé ben Yo'ezer of Zeredah said: Let your house be a meeting-place for scholars; sit at their feet in the dust, and drink in their words thirstingly.

5. Yosé ben Yoḥanan of Jerusalem said: Let your house be wide open [to strangers]; treat the poor as members of your own family; and do not gossip with women. This has been said even with regard to one's own wife, how much more does it apply to another man's wife. Hence the sages say: Whoever gossips with women brings harm to himself, for he neglects the study of the Torah and will in the end inherit *Gehinnom.*

6. Joshua ben Peraḥyah and Nittai of Arbel received the oral tradition from the preceding. Joshua ben Peraḥyah said: Provide yourself with a teacher; get yourself a companion; and judge all men favorably.

7. Nittai of Arbel said: Keep aloof from a bad neighbor; do not associate with an evil man; and do not give up the belief in retribution [wickedness will not succeed in the end].

8. Judah ben Tabbai and Simeon ben Shataḥ received the oral tradition from the preceding. Judah ben Tabbai said: Do not [as a judge] play the part of a counselor; when the parties in a lawsuit are standing before you, regard them both as guilty; but when they go away from you, after having submitted to the judgment, regard them both as innocent.

9. Simeon ben Shataḥ said: Examine the witnesses thoroughly; be careful with your words, lest through them the witnesses learn to give false testimony.

10. Shemayah and Avtalyon received the oral tradition from the preceding. Shemayah said: Love work; hate the holding of public office; and do not be intimate with the ruling authorities.

גיהנם the place of punishment in the hereafter. גיא בן־הנם is mentioned in Jeremiah 32:35 as the valley of Ben-Hinnom, near Jerusalem, where idolators used to sacrifice human lives. The valley of Hinnom became identified with woe and suffering as a result of the horrible crimes committed in it.

יהיו בעיניך כרשעים that is, the judge should be impartial; he must not look upon either litigant with favor, but should regard both sides with equal suspicion.

שמעון בן שטח, brother of queen Salome Alexandra, laid the foundations of an elementary school system among the Jews in the beginning of the first century before the common era.

שמעיה ואבטליון are said to have been descendants of proselytes.

יא. אַבְטַלְיוֹן אוֹמֵר: חֲכָמִים, הִזָּהֲרוּ בְדִבְרֵיכֶם, שֶׁמָּא תָחוֹבוּ חוֹבַת גָּלוּת וְתִגְלוּ לִמְקוֹם מַיִם הָרָעִים, וְיִשְׁתּוּ הַתַּלְמִידִים הַבָּאִים אַחֲרֵיכֶם וְיָמוּתוּ, וְנִמְצָא שֵׁם שָׁמַיִם מִתְחַלֵּל.

יב. הִלֵּל וְשַׁמַּי קִבְּלוּ מֵהֶם. הִלֵּל אוֹמֵר: הֱוֵי מִתַּלְמִידָיו שֶׁל אַהֲרֹן: אוֹהֵב שָׁלוֹם וְרוֹדֵף שָׁלוֹם, אוֹהֵב אֶת הַבְּרִיּוֹת וּמְקָרְבָן לַתּוֹרָה.

יג. הוּא הָיָה אוֹמֵר: נְגַד שְׁמָא אֲבַד שְׁמֵהּ, וּדְלָא מוֹסִיף יָסֵף, וּדְלָא יָלֵף קְטָלָא חַיָּב, וּדְאִשְׁתַּמַּשׁ בְּתָגָא חֲלָף.

יד. הוּא הָיָה אוֹמֵר: אִם אֵין אֲנִי לִי, מִי לִי; וּכְשֶׁאֲנִי לְעַצְמִי, מָה אֲנִי; וְאִם לֹא עַכְשָׁו, אֵימָתָי.

טו. שַׁמַּי אוֹמֵר: עֲשֵׂה תוֹרָתְךָ קֶבַע, אֱמֹר מְעַט וַעֲשֵׂה הַרְבֵּה, וֶהֱוֵי מְקַבֵּל אֶת כָּל הָאָדָם בְּסֵבֶר פָּנִים יָפוֹת.

טז. רַבָּן גַּמְלִיאֵל אוֹמֵר: עֲשֵׂה לְךָ רַב, וְהִסְתַּלֵּק מִן הַסָּפֵק, וְאַל תַּרְבֶּה לְעַשֵּׂר אֲמָדוֹת.

יז. שִׁמְעוֹן בְּנוֹ אוֹמֵר: כָּל יָמַי גָּדַלְתִּי בֵּין הַחֲכָמִים וְלֹא מָצָאתִי לַגּוּף טוֹב מִשְּׁתִיקָה, וְלֹא הַמִּדְרָשׁ עִקָּר אֶלָּא הַמַּעֲשֶׂה, וְכָל הַמַּרְבֶּה דְבָרִים מֵבִיא חֵטְא.

יח. רַבָּן שִׁמְעוֹן בֶּן גַּמְלִיאֵל אוֹמֵר: עַל שְׁלֹשָׁה דְבָרִים הָעוֹלָם קַיָּם: עַל הָאֱמֶת, וְעַל הַדִּין, וְעַל הַשָּׁלוֹם, שֶׁנֶּאֱמַר: אֱמֶת וּמִשְׁפַּט שָׁלוֹם שִׁפְטוּ בְּשַׁעֲרֵיכֶם.

הזהרו בדבריכם Teachers are cautioned against their use of inexact language which might bring their students under the influence of heresy.

הלל ושמאי flourished in Jerusalem a few decades before the common era. The last of the five *Zugoth*, they are regarded as the first of the *Tannaim* whose interpretations of biblical law and oral tradition are recorded in the Mishnah, Tosefta, and other works. In contrast to Shammai, Hillel was

11.   Avtalyon said: Scholars, be careful with your words! You may incur the penalty of exile and be banished to a place of evil waters [heretical teachings], and the disciples who follow you into exile are likely to drink of them and die [a spiritual death], with the result that the name of Heaven would be profaned.

12.   Hillel and Shammai received the oral tradition from the preceding. Hillel said: Be of the disciples of Aaron, loving peace and pursuing peace; be one who loves his fellow men and draws them near to the Torah.

13.   He used to say: He who seeks greater reputation loses his reputation; he who does not increase his knowledge decreases it; he who does not study deserves death; he who makes unworthy use of the crown [of learning] shall perish.

14.   He used to say: If I am not for myself, who is for me? If I care only for myself, what am I? If not now, when?

15.   Shammai said: Make your study of the Torah a regular habit; say little but do much; and receive all men cheerfully.

16.   Rabban Gamaliel said: Provide yourself with a teacher and avoid doubt; and do not make a habit of giving tithes by guesswork.

17.   Simeon his son said: All my life I have been brought up among the sages, and I have found nothing better for a person than silence; study is not the most important thing but practice; and whoever talks too much brings about sin.

18.   Rabban Simeon ben Gamaliel said: The world is established on three principles: truth, justice, and peace, as it is said: "You shall administer truth, justice and peace within your gates."[1]

---

famous for his meek and gentle disposition. They were the founders of the schools named after them: *Beth Hillel* and *Beth Shammai*.

. . . אם אין אני לי that is, one must be self-reliant, but must not live for himself. אם לא עכשיו אימתי one must take swift advantage of opportunity.

רבן גמליאל was a grandson of Hillel. He was the first to be known by the title *Rabban* ("Master"), given to the heads of the Sanhedrin. Like Hillel, he is also known by the title *Zaken* ("Elder"). He lived shortly before the Second Temple was destroyed.

ואל תרבה לעשר אומדות that is, keep clear of all doubt. Even when you come to pay the tenth part of your annual income for charitable uses, let there be no doubt that what you pay represents really a tenth of your income.

[1] *Zechariah* 8:16.

רַבִּי חֲנַנְיָא בֶּן עֲקַשְׁיָא אוֹמֵר: רָצָה הַקָּדוֹשׁ בָּרוּךְ הוּא
לְזַכּוֹת אֶת יִשְׂרָאֵל, לְפִיכָךְ הִרְבָּה לָהֶם תּוֹרָה וּמִצְוֹת, שֶׁנֶּאֱמַר:
יְיָ חָפֵץ לְמַעַן צִדְקוֹ, יַגְדִּיל תּוֹרָה וְיַאְדִּיר.

פֶּרֶק שֵׁנִי

כָּל יִשְׂרָאֵל יֵשׁ לָהֶם חֵלֶק לָעוֹלָם הַבָּא, שֶׁנֶּאֱמַר, וְעַמֵּךְ
כֻּלָּם צַדִּיקִים, לְעוֹלָם יִירְשׁוּ אָרֶץ; נֵצֶר מַטָּעַי, מַעֲשֵׂה יָדַי
לְהִתְפָּאֵר.

א. רַבִּי אוֹמֵר: אֵיזוֹ הִיא דֶרֶךְ יְשָׁרָה שֶׁיָּבוֹר לוֹ הָאָדָם,
כָּל שֶׁהִיא תִפְאֶרֶת לְעֹשֶׂהָ וְתִפְאֶרֶת לוֹ מִן הָאָדָם; וֶהֱוֵי זָהִיר
בְּמִצְוָה קַלָּה כְּבַחֲמוּרָה, שֶׁאֵין אַתָּה יוֹדֵעַ מַתַּן שְׂכָרָן שֶׁל
מִצְוֹת; וֶהֱוֵי מְחַשֵּׁב הֶפְסֵד מִצְוָה כְּנֶגֶד שְׂכָרָהּ, וּשְׂכַר עֲבֵרָה
כְּנֶגֶד הֶפְסֵדָהּ. הִסְתַּכֵּל בִּשְׁלֹשָׁה דְבָרִים וְאֵין אַתָּה בָא לִידֵי
עֲבֵרָה: דַּע מַה לְמַעְלָה מִמְּךָ, עַיִן רוֹאָה, וְאֹזֶן שׁוֹמַעַת, וְכָל
מַעֲשֶׂיךָ בַּסֵּפֶר נִכְתָּבִים.

ב. רַבָּן גַּמְלִיאֵל בְּנוֹ שֶׁל רַבִּי יְהוּדָה הַנָּשִׂיא אוֹמֵר: יָפֶה
תַלְמוּד תּוֹרָה עִם דֶּרֶךְ אֶרֶץ, שֶׁיְּגִיעַת שְׁנֵיהֶם מַשְׁכַּחַת עָוֹן;
וְכָל תּוֹרָה שֶׁאֵין עִמָּהּ מְלָאכָה סוֹפָהּ בְּטֵלָה וְגוֹרֶרֶת עָוֹן; וְכָל
הָעוֹסְקִים עִם הַצִּבּוּר יִהְיוּ עוֹסְקִים עִמָּהֶם לְשֵׁם שָׁמַיִם, שֶׁזְּכוּת
אֲבוֹתָם מְסַיַּעְתָּם וְצִדְקָתָם עוֹמֶדֶת לָעַד. וְאַתֶּם, מַעֲלֶה אֲנִי
עֲלֵיכֶם שָׂכָר הַרְבֵּה כְּאִלּוּ עֲשִׂיתֶם.

רבי חנניא belonged to the third generation of the *Tannaim*, and flourished
in the middle of the second century. His dictum, which is added in the Prayerbook at the end of each chapter of *Avoth*, is an excerpt from Mishnah Makkoth 3:16.

רבי is sometimes called *Rabbenu ha-Kadosh* ("our saintly teacher"). All
the best qualities were combined in him. He is said to have been born in 135,
when Rabbi Akiba died. He lived to be 84 years old. Famous as the compiler

Rabbi Ḥananyah ben Akashyah said: The Holy One, blessed be he, desired to purify Israel; hence he gave them a Torah rich in rules of conduct, as it is said: "The Lord was pleased, for the sake of [Israel's] righteousness, to render the Torah great and glorious."[1]

CHAPTER TWO

All Israel have a share in the world to come, as it is said: "Your people shall all be righteous; they shall possess the land forever; they are a plant of my own, the work of my hands, wherein I may glory."[2]

1. Rabbi [Judah ha-Nasi] said: Which is the right course that a man should choose for himself? One which is creditable to the person adopting it, and on account of which he gains respect from men. Be careful to perform a minor *mitzvah* just as well as a major one, for you do not know the reward for each *mitzvah*. Balance the loss sustained by the performance of a *mitzvah* against the reward secured by its observance, and the profit of a sin against its injury. Consider three things and you will not come into the grip of sin—know what is above you: a seeing eye, a hearing ear, and a book in which all your deeds are recorded.

2. Rabban Gamaliel, the son of Rabbi Judah ha-Nasi, said: It is well to combine Torah study with some worldly occupation, for the energy taken up by both of them keeps sin out of one's mind; all Torah study which is not combined with some trade must at length fail and occasion sin. Let all who work for the community do so from a spiritual motive, for then the merit of their fathers will sustain them, and their righteousness will endure forever. "I credit you with great reward [God says] as if you accomplished it all."

---

and editor of the Mishnah, he was without a rival among his contemporaries in learning. He said: "I learned much from my teachers, more from my colleagues, and most of all from my pupils" (Makkoth 10a). He possessed great wealth of which he gave freely to poor scholars. The greatest scholar of the period, he was designated simply *Rabbi* ("Master") par excellence. A descendant of Hillel in the seventh generation, he is also known as Judah ha-Nasi (head of the Sanhedrin).

רבן גמליאל the third, who belonged to the last generation of the *Tannaim*. He succeeded his father in the office of *Nasi* in the third century.

צורת עין that is, one would be driven to dishonest means of obtaining a livelihood.

---

[1] *Isaiah* 42:21.　[2] *Isaiah* 60:21.

ג. הֱווּ זְהִירִין בָּרָשׁוּת, שֶׁאֵין מְקָרְבִין לוֹ לְאָדָם אֶלָּא לְצֹרֶךְ עַצְמָן; נִרְאִין כְּאוֹהֲבִין בִּשְׁעַת הֲנָאָתָן, וְאֵין עוֹמְדִין לוֹ לְאָדָם בִּשְׁעַת דָּחֳקוֹ.

ד. הוּא הָיָה אוֹמֵר: עֲשֵׂה רְצוֹנוֹ כִּרְצוֹנֶךָ, כְּדֵי שֶׁיַּעֲשֶׂה רְצוֹנְךָ כִּרְצוֹנוֹ; בַּטֵּל רְצוֹנְךָ מִפְּנֵי רְצוֹנוֹ, כְּדֵי שֶׁיְּבַטֵּל רְצוֹן אֲחֵרִים מִפְּנֵי רְצוֹנֶךָ.

ה. הַלֵּל אוֹמֵר: אַל תִּפְרוֹשׁ מִן הַצִּבּוּר; וְאַל תַּאֲמֵן בְּעַצְמְךָ עַד יוֹם מוֹתְךָ; וְאַל תָּדִין אֶת חֲבֵרְךָ עַד שֶׁתַּגִּיעַ לִמְקוֹמוֹ; וְאַל תֹּאמַר דָּבָר שֶׁאִי אֶפְשָׁר לִשְׁמֹעַ שֶׁסּוֹפוֹ לְהִשָּׁמַע; וְאַל תֹּאמַר לִכְשֶׁאֶפָּנֶה אֶשְׁנֶה, שֶׁמָּא לֹא תִפָּנֶה.

ו. הוּא הָיָה אוֹמֵר: אֵין בּוּר יְרֵא חֵטְא, וְלֹא עַם הָאָרֶץ חָסִיד, וְלֹא הַבַּיְשָׁן לָמֵד, וְלֹא הַקַּפְּדָן מְלַמֵּד, וְלֹא כָל הַמַּרְבֶּה בִסְחוֹרָה מַחְכִּים; וּבַמָּקוֹם שֶׁאֵין אֲנָשִׁים הִשְׁתַּדֵּל לִהְיוֹת אִישׁ.

ז. אַף הוּא רָאָה גֻּלְגֹּלֶת אַחַת שֶׁצָּפָה עַל פְּנֵי הַמָּיִם. אָמַר לָהּ: עַל דַּאֲטֵיפְתְּ אַטִיפוּךְ, וְסוֹף מְטַיְפָיִךְ יְטוּפוּן.

ח. הוּא הָיָה אוֹמֵר: מַרְבֶּה בָשָׂר, מַרְבֶּה רִמָּה; מַרְבֶּה נְכָסִים, מַרְבֶּה דְאָנָה; מַרְבֶּה נָשִׁים, מַרְבֶּה כְשָׁפִים; מַרְבֶּה שְׁפָחוֹת, מַרְבֶּה זִמָּה; מַרְבֶּה עֲבָדִים, מַרְבֶּה גָזֵל. מַרְבֶּה תוֹרָה, מַרְבֶּה חַיִּים; מַרְבֶּה יְשִׁיבָה, מַרְבֶּה חָכְמָה; מַרְבֶּה עֵצָה, מַרְבֶּה תְבוּנָה; מַרְבֶּה צְדָקָה, מַרְבֶּה שָׁלוֹם. קָנָה שֵׁם טוֹב, קָנָה לְעַצְמוֹ; קָנָה לוֹ דִבְרֵי תוֹרָה, קָנָה לוֹ חַיֵּי הָעוֹלָם הַבָּא.

שאי אפשר לשמוע is read by Rashi שאפשר לשמוע in the sense that one should take swift advantage of each opportunity to acquire knowledge.

3. Be cautious of the ruling authorities, for they befriend a man only for their own interests; they appear as friends when it is to their own advantage, but they do not stand by a man when he is in distress.

4. He used to say: Do God's will as you would do your own will, so that he may do your will as if it were his; sacrifice your will for the sake of his will, so that he may undo the will of others before yours.

5. Hillel said: Do not keep aloof from the community; be not sure of yourself till the day of your death; do not judge your fellow man until you have been in his position; do not say anything which cannot be understood at once, in the hope that ultimately it will be understood; and do not say: "When I shall have leisure I shall study," for you may never have leisure.

6. He used to say: An empty-headed man cannot be sin-fearing, nor can an ignorant person be pious; the bashful cannot learn, nor can the quick-tempered teach; nor can anyone who is engrossed in trade become a scholar; and in a place where there are no men, strive to be a man.

7. He saw a skull floating on the surface of the water. He said to it: Because you drowned others, others have drowned you; and those who have drowned you shall themselves be drowned [measure for measure].

8. He used to say: The more flesh, the more worms [in the grave]; the more property, the more anxiety; the more wives, the more witchcraft; the more female servants, the more lewdness; the more male servants, the more thievery; but the more Torah study, the more life; the more schooling, the more wisdom; the more counsel, the more understanding; the more righteousness, the more peace. One who has acquired a good name, has acquired it for himself; one who has acquired for himself Torah has acquired for himself the life of the world to come.

בור a man devoid of both knowledge and moral principles. This term originally signifies a piece of land completely uncultivated.

מרבה כשפים Rival wives often resorted to black magic in their efforts to retain their husband's affection.

ט. רַבָּן יוֹחָנָן בֶּן זַכַּי קִבֵּל מֵהִלֵּל וּמִשַּׁמַּאי. הוּא הָיָה אוֹמֵר: אִם לָמַדְתָּ תוֹרָה הַרְבֵּה, אַל תַּחֲזִק טוֹבָה לְעַצְמֶךָ, כִּי לְכָךְ נוֹצָרְתָּ.

י. חֲמִשָּׁה תַלְמִידִים הָיוּ לוֹ לְרַבָּן יוֹחָנָן בֶּן זַכַּי, וְאֵלּוּ הֵן: רַבִּי אֱלִיעֶזֶר בֶּן הוֹרְקָנוֹס, רַבִּי יְהוֹשֻׁעַ בֶּן חֲנַנְיָא, רַבִּי יוֹסֵי הַכֹּהֵן, רַבִּי שִׁמְעוֹן בֶּן נְתַנְאֵל, וְרַבִּי אֶלְעָזָר בֶּן עֲרָךְ.

יא. הוּא הָיָה מוֹנֶה שְׁבָחָם: רַבִּי אֱלִיעֶזֶר בֶּן הוֹרְקָנוֹס בּוֹר סוּד, שֶׁאֵינוֹ מְאַבֵּד טִפָּה; רַבִּי יְהוֹשֻׁעַ בֶּן חֲנַנְיָא, אַשְׁרֵי יוֹלַדְתּוֹ; רַבִּי יוֹסֵי הַכֹּהֵן חָסִיד; רַבִּי שִׁמְעוֹן בֶּן נְתַנְאֵל יְרֵא חֵטְא; וְרַבִּי אֶלְעָזָר בֶּן עֲרָךְ כְּמַעְיָן הַמִּתְגַּבֵּר.

יב. הוּא הָיָה אוֹמֵר: אִם יִהְיוּ כָּל חַכְמֵי יִשְׂרָאֵל בְּכַף מֹאזְנַיִם, וֶאֱלִיעֶזֶר בֶּן הוֹרְקָנוֹס בְּכַף שְׁנִיָּה, מַכְרִיעַ אֶת כֻּלָּם. אַבָּא שָׁאוּל אוֹמֵר מִשְּׁמוֹ: אִם יִהְיוּ כָּל חַכְמֵי יִשְׂרָאֵל בְּכַף מֹאזְנַיִם, וֶאֱלִיעֶזֶר בֶּן הוֹרְקָנוֹס אַף עִמָּהֶם, וְאֶלְעָזָר בֶּן עֲרָךְ בְּכַף שְׁנִיָּה, מַכְרִיעַ אֶת כֻּלָּם.

יג. אָמַר לָהֶם: צְאוּ וּרְאוּ אֵיזוֹ הִיא דֶּרֶךְ טוֹבָה שֶׁיִּדְבַּק בָּהּ הָאָדָם. רַבִּי אֱלִיעֶזֶר אוֹמֵר: עַיִן טוֹבָה. רַבִּי יְהוֹשֻׁעַ אוֹמֵר: חָבֵר טוֹב. רַבִּי יוֹסֵי אוֹמֵר: שָׁכֵן טוֹב. רַבִּי שִׁמְעוֹן אוֹמֵר: הָרוֹאֶה אֶת הַנּוֹלָד. רַבִּי אֶלְעָזָר אוֹמֵר: לֵב טוֹב. אָמַר לָהֶם: רוֹאֶה אֲנִי אֶת דִּבְרֵי אֶלְעָזָר בֶּן עֲרָךְ מִדִּבְרֵיכֶם, שֶׁבִּכְלַל דְּבָרָיו דִּבְרֵיכֶם.

יוחנן בן זכאי saved the nation from disintegration after the destruction of the Temple when he reorganized the Sanhedrin in Yavneh, south of Jaffa. According to tradition, he died at the age of 120.

אליעזר בן הורקנוס is frequently quoted in the Mishnah. Against the wishes of his father who threatened to disinherit him, he began to study late in life and developed into the greatest scholar of the period. Though a brother-in-

9. Rabban Yoḥanan ben Zakkai received the oral tradition from Hillel and Shammai. He used to say: If you have learnt much Torah, do not claim credit for yourself, because you were created for this purpose.

10. Rabban Yoḥanan ben Zakkai had five pre-eminent disciples, namely: Rabbi Eliezer ben Hyrcanus, Rabbi Joshua ben Ḥananyah, Rabbi Yosé the Priest, Rabbi Simeon ben Nethanel, and Rabbi Elazar ben Arakh.

11. He used to sum up their merits: Eliezer ben Hyrcanus is a cemented cistern which loses not a drop [retentive memory]; Joshua ben Ḥananyah—happy is his mother; Yosé the Priest is most pious; Simeon ben Nethanel is one who fears sin; Elazar ben Arakh is like a spring that ever gathers force [creative mind].

12. He used to say: If all the sages of Israel were in one scale of the balance, and Eliezer ben Hyrcanus in the other, he would outweigh them all. Abba Saul, however, quoted him otherwise: If all the sages of Israel, including Eliezer ben Hyrcanus, were in one scale of the balance, and Elazar ben Arakh in the other, he would outweigh them all [originality surpasses retentiveness].

13. He [Yoḥanan ben Zakkai] said to them: Go and see which is the best quality to which a man should cling. Rabbi Eliezer said: A good eye [generosity]; Rabbi Joshua said: A good friend [friendliness]; Rabbi Yosé said: A good neighbor [goodwill]; Rabbi Simeon said: One who considers the probable consequences [foresight]; Rabbi Elazar said: A good heart [unselfishness]. Said he to them: I prefer what Elazar ben Arakh has said to what you have said, because in his words yours are included.

---

law of Gamaliel II, the president of the Sanhedrin, he was excommunicated by his colleagues because he refused to accept the decision of the majority on a point of law that arose for discussion. He is sometimes spoken of as "Rabbi Eliezer the Great."

אשרי יולדתו Great credit for his scholarship was due to his mother, who is said to have taken him as an infant to the academy of learning so that his ears might become attuned to the sound of Torah. Rabbi Joshua ben Ḥananyah successfully debated with Greek philosophers and was famous as the representative of Jewish wit and wisdom.

אבא ("father") is not part of this *Tanna's* name, but a title. Abba Saul lived during the second century.

יד. אָמַר לָהֶם: צְאוּ וּרְאוּ אֵיזוֹ הִיא דֶרֶךְ רָעָה שֶׁיִּתְרַחֵק
מִמֶּנָּה הָאָדָם. רַבִּי אֱלִיעֶזֶר אוֹמֵר: עַיִן רָעָה. רַבִּי יְהוֹשֻׁעַ
אוֹמֵר: חָבֵר רָע. רַבִּי יוֹסֵי אוֹמֵר: שָׁכֵן רָע. רַבִּי שִׁמְעוֹן אוֹמֵר:
הַלֹּוֶה וְאֵינוֹ מְשַׁלֵּם; אֶחָד הַלֹּוֶה מִן הָאָדָם כְּלֹוֶה מִן הַמָּקוֹם,
שֶׁנֶּאֱמַר: לֹוֶה רָשָׁע וְלֹא יְשַׁלֵּם, וְצַדִּיק חוֹנֵן וְנוֹתֵן. רַבִּי אֶלְעָזָר
אוֹמֵר: לֵב רָע. אָמַר לָהֶם: רוֹאֶה אֲנִי אֶת דִּבְרֵי אֶלְעָזָר בֶּן
עֲרָךְ מִדִּבְרֵיכֶם, שֶׁבִּכְלַל דְּבָרָיו דִּבְרֵיכֶם.

טו. הֵם אָמְרוּ שְׁלֹשָׁה דְּבָרִים. רַבִּי אֱלִיעֶזֶר אוֹמֵר: יְהִי
כְבוֹד חֲבֵרְךָ חָבִיב עָלֶיךָ כְּשֶׁלָּךְ, וְאַל תְּהִי נוֹחַ לִכְעוֹס, וְשׁוּב
יוֹם אֶחָד לִפְנֵי מִיתָתְךָ. וֶהֱוֵי מִתְחַמֵּם כְּנֶגֶד אוּרָן שֶׁל חֲכָמִים,
וֶהֱוֵי זָהִיר בְּגַחַלְתָּן שֶׁלֹּא תִכָּוֶה, שֶׁנְּשִׁיכָתָן נְשִׁיכַת שׁוּעָל,
וַעֲקִיצָתָן עֲקִיצַת עַקְרָב, וּלְחִישָׁתָן לְחִישַׁת שָׂרָף, וְכָל דִּבְרֵיהֶם
כְּגַחֲלֵי אֵשׁ.

טז. רַבִּי יְהוֹשֻׁעַ אוֹמֵר: עַיִן הָרָע וְיֵצֶר הָרָע וְשִׂנְאַת הַבְּרִיּוֹת
מוֹצִיאִים אֶת הָאָדָם מִן הָעוֹלָם.

יז. רַבִּי יוֹסֵי אוֹמֵר: יְהִי מָמוֹן חֲבֵרְךָ חָבִיב עָלֶיךָ כְּשֶׁלָּךְ,
וְהַתְקֵן עַצְמְךָ לִלְמוֹד תּוֹרָה שֶׁאֵינָהּ יְרֻשָּׁה לָךְ, וְכָל מַעֲשֶׂיךָ
יִהְיוּ לְשֵׁם שָׁמָיִם.

יח. רַבִּי שִׁמְעוֹן אוֹמֵר: הֱוֵי זָהִיר בִּקְרִיאַת שְׁמַע וּבִתְפִלָּה;
וּכְשֶׁאַתָּה מִתְפַּלֵּל, אַל תַּעַשׂ תְּפִלָּתְךָ קֶבַע אֶלָּא רַחֲמִים
וְתַחֲנוּנִים לִפְנֵי הַמָּקוֹם, שֶׁנֶּאֱמַר: כִּי חַנּוּן וְרַחוּם הוּא, אֶרֶךְ
אַפַּיִם וְרַב חֶסֶד וְנִחָם עַל הָרָעָה; וְאַל תְּהִי רָשָׁע בִּפְנֵי עַצְמֶךָ.

כלוה מן המקום Since all wealth belongs to God, the borrower is considered
as borrowing directly from God, the Righteous One, who will repay the bene-
volent lender what the debtor fails to repay.

14.   He further said to them: Go and see which is the worst quality a man should shun. Rabbi Eliezer said: An evil eye [greed]; Rabbi Joshua said: A bad friend [hatred]; Rabbi Yosé said: A bad neighbor [discord]; Rabbi Simeon said: One who borrows and does not repay. It is the same whether one borrows from man or from God, as it is said: "The wicked borrows and repays not, but the righteous deals graciously and gives."[1] Rabbi Elazar said: An evil heart [selfishness]. Said he to them: I prefer what Elazar ben Arakh has said to what you have said, for in his words yours are included.

15.   They each said three things. Rabbi Eliezer said: Let your friend's honor be as dear to you as your own; be not easily provoked to anger; repent one day before your death [every day, for you may die tomorrow]. He further said: Warm yourself by the fire of the scholars, but beware of their glowing coals [treat them respectfully], lest you burn yourself; for the bite of scholars is as hurtful as that of a fox, their sting is as deadly as that of a scorpion, their hiss is like that of a serpent, and all their words are like coals of fire [and should be heeded].

16.   Rabbi Joshua said: The evil eye [greed], the evil impulse and hatred of mankind shorten a man's life.

17.   Rabbi Yosé said: Let your friend's property be as precious to you as your own; give yourself to studying the Torah, for it does not come to you by inheritance; and let all your deeds be done in the name of Heaven.

18.   Rabbi Simeon said: Be careful in reading the *Shema* and the *Shemoneh Esreh*; when you pray, do not regard your prayer as a perfunctory act, but as a plea for mercy and grace before God, as it is said: "For he is gracious and merciful, slow to anger, abounding in kindness, and relenting of evil."[2] Do not be wicked in your own esteem [lest you set yourself a low standard of conduct].

לשם שמים for the sake of God, that is, with pure purpose and good intentions.

קריאת שמע and all regularly repeated prayers should never be recited in a mechanical manner, without understanding and a devotional frame of mind.

---

[1] *Psalm* 37:21.   [2] *Joel* 2:13.

יט. רַבִּי אֶלְעָזָר אוֹמֵר: הֱוֵי שָׁקוּד לִלְמֹד תּוֹרָה, וְדַע מַה שֶּׁתָּשִׁיב לְאֶפִּיקוֹרוֹס, וְדַע לִפְנֵי מִי אַתָּה עָמֵל וּמִי הוּא בַּעַל מְלַאכְתְּךָ שֶׁיְּשַׁלֶּם־לָךְ שְׂכַר פְּעֻלָּתֶךָ.

כ. רַבִּי טַרְפוֹן אוֹמֵר: הַיּוֹם קָצֵר, וְהַמְּלָאכָה מְרֻבָּה, וְהַפּוֹעֲלִים עֲצֵלִים, וְהַשָּׂכָר הַרְבֵּה, וּבַעַל הַבַּיִת דּוֹחֵק.

כא. הוּא הָיָה אוֹמֵר: לֹא עָלֶיךָ הַמְּלָאכָה לִגְמֹר, וְלֹא אַתָּה בֶּן חוֹרִין לְהִבָּטֵל מִמֶּנָּה. אִם לָמַדְתָּ תּוֹרָה הַרְבֵּה, נוֹתְנִים לָךְ שָׂכָר הַרְבֵּה, וְנֶאֱמָן הוּא בַּעַל מְלַאכְתְּךָ שֶׁיְּשַׁלֶּם־לָךְ שְׂכַר פְּעֻלָּתֶךָ; וְדַע שֶׁמַּתַּן שְׂכָרָן שֶׁל צַדִּיקִים לֶעָתִיד לָבוֹא.

רַבִּי חֲנַנְיָא בֶּן עֲקַשְׁיָא אוֹמֵר: רָצָה הַקָּדוֹשׁ בָּרוּךְ הוּא לְזַכּוֹת אֶת יִשְׂרָאֵל, לְפִיכָךְ הִרְבָּה לָהֶם תּוֹרָה וּמִצְוֹת, שֶׁנֶּאֱמַר: יְיָ חָפֵץ לְמַעַן צִדְקוֹ, יַגְדִּיל תּוֹרָה וְיַאְדִּיר.

פֶּרֶק שְׁלִישִׁי

כָּל יִשְׂרָאֵל יֵשׁ לָהֶם חֵלֶק לָעוֹלָם הַבָּא, שֶׁנֶּאֱמַר: וְעַמֵּךְ כֻּלָּם צַדִּיקִים, לְעוֹלָם יִירְשׁוּ אָרֶץ; נֵצֶר מַטָּעַי, מַעֲשֵׂה יָדַי לְהִתְפָּאֵר.

א. עֲקַבְיָא בֶּן מַהֲלַלְאֵל אוֹמֵר: הִסְתַּכֵּל בִּשְׁלֹשָׁה דְבָרִים וְאֵין אַתָּה בָא לִידֵי עֲבֵרָה: דַּע מֵאַיִן בָּאתָ, וּלְאָן אַתָּה הוֹלֵךְ, וְלִפְנֵי מִי אַתָּה עָתִיד לִתֵּן דִּין וְחֶשְׁבּוֹן. מֵאַיִן בָּאתָ, מִטִּפָּה סְרוּחָה; וּלְאָן אַתָּה הוֹלֵךְ, לִמְקוֹם עָפָר, רִמָּה וְתוֹלֵעָה; וְלִפְנֵי מִי אַתָּה עָתִיד לִתֵּן דִּין וְחֶשְׁבּוֹן, לִפְנֵי מֶלֶךְ מַלְכֵי הַמְּלָכִים, הַקָּדוֹשׁ בָּרוּךְ הוּא.

רבי טרפון was a contemporary of Rabban Yoḥanan ben Zakkai and a colleague of Rabbi Akiba. He used his great wealth for charitable purposes.

19. Rabbi Elazar said: Be eager to study the Torah; know what to answer an unbeliever; know before whom you toil, who your Employer is, who will pay you the reward of your labor.

20. Rabbi Tarfon said: The day [life] is short; the task is great; the workmen [human beings] are lazy; the reward is great, and the Master is insistent.

21. He used to say: You are not called upon to complete the work [of Torah study], yet you are not free to evade it; if you have studied much Torah, much reward will be given you—your Employer can be trusted to pay you for your work; and know that the grant of reward to the righteous will be in the time to come.

Rabbi Ḥananyah ben Akashyah said: The Holy One, blessed be he, desired to purify Israel; hence he gave them a Torah rich in rules of conduct, as it is said: "The Lord was pleased, for the sake of [Israel's] righteousness, to render the Torah great and glorious."[1]

CHAPTER THREE

All Israel have a share in the world to come, as it is said: "Your people shall all be righteous; they shall possess the land forever; they are a plant of my own, the work of my hands, wherein I may glory."[2]

1. Akavyah ben Mahalalel said: Reflect on three things and you will not come into the grip of sin: know whence you came, whither you are going, and before whom you are destined to give a strict account. *Whence you came*—from a malodorous drop; *whither you are going*—to a place of dust, worms and moths; *and before whom you are destined to give a strict account*—before the supreme King of kings, the Holy One, blessed be he.

אפיקורוס a follower of Epicurus, the Greek philosopher who taught that "all parts of the universe . . . owe their origin to accident and chance" (Maimonides, *Guide*, III, 17). Because of the phonetic resemblance between אפיקורוס and פקר ("to be licentious") the term *epikurus* is used in talmudic literature to denote one who denies the authority of the Torah. There is a statement that he who insults a scholar is an *epikurus* (Sanhedrin 99b).

עקביא בן מהללאל was a contemporary of Hillel. On Shammai's death he was offered the position of vice-president of the Sanhedrin on condition that he first change his views on certain points of law, but he refused.

---

[1] *Isaiah* 42:21.   [2] *Isaiah* 60:21.

ב. רַבִּי חֲנִינָא סְגַן הַכֹּהֲנִים אוֹמֵר: הֱוֵי מִתְפַּלֵּל בִּשְׁלוֹמָהּ שֶׁל מַלְכוּת, שֶׁאִלְמָלֵא מוֹרָאָהּ אִישׁ אֶת רֵעֵהוּ חַיִּים בְּלָעוֹ.

ג. רַבִּי חֲנַנְיָא בֶּן תְּרַדְיוֹן אוֹמֵר: שְׁנַיִם שֶׁיּוֹשְׁבִים וְאֵין בֵּינֵיהֶם דִּבְרֵי תוֹרָה, הֲרֵי זֶה מוֹשַׁב לֵצִים, שֶׁנֶּאֱמַר: וּבְמוֹשַׁב לֵצִים לֹא יָשָׁב. אֲבָל שְׁנַיִם שֶׁיּוֹשְׁבִים וְיֵשׁ בֵּינֵיהֶם דִּבְרֵי תוֹרָה, שְׁכִינָה שְׁרוּיָה בֵינֵיהֶם, שֶׁנֶּאֱמַר: אָז נִדְבְּרוּ יִרְאֵי יְיָ אִישׁ אֶל רֵעֵהוּ, וַיַּקְשֵׁב יְיָ וַיִּשְׁמָע, וַיִּכָּתֵב סֵפֶר זִכָּרוֹן לְפָנָיו, לְיִרְאֵי יְיָ וּלְחֹשְׁבֵי שְׁמוֹ. אֵין לִי אֶלָּא שְׁנַיִם, מִנַּיִן אֲפִילוּ אֶחָד שֶׁיּוֹשֵׁב וְעוֹסֵק בַּתּוֹרָה, שֶׁהַקָּדוֹשׁ בָּרוּךְ הוּא קוֹבֵעַ לוֹ שָׂכָר, שֶׁנֶּאֱמַר: יֵשֵׁב בָּדָד וְיִדֹּם כִּי נָטַל עָלָיו.

ד. רַבִּי שִׁמְעוֹן אוֹמֵר: שְׁלשָׁה שֶׁאָכְלוּ עַל שֻׁלְחָן אֶחָד וְלֹא אָמְרוּ עָלָיו דִּבְרֵי תוֹרָה, כְּאִלּוּ אָכְלוּ מִזִּבְחֵי מֵתִים, שֶׁנֶּאֱמַר: כִּי כָּל שֻׁלְחָנוֹת מָלְאוּ קִיא צֹאָה בְּלִי מָקוֹם. אֲבָל שְׁלשָׁה שֶׁאָכְלוּ עַל שֻׁלְחָן אֶחָד וְאָמְרוּ עָלָיו דִּבְרֵי תוֹרָה, כְּאִלּוּ אָכְלוּ מִשֻּׁלְחָנוֹ שֶׁל מָקוֹם, שֶׁנֶּאֱמַר: וַיְדַבֵּר אֵלַי, זֶה הַשֻּׁלְחָן אֲשֶׁר לִפְנֵי יְיָ.

ה. רַבִּי חֲנִינָא בֶּן חֲכִינַי אוֹמֵר: הַנֵּעוֹר בַּלַּיְלָה וְהַמְהַלֵּךְ בַּדֶּרֶךְ יְחִידִי וּמְפַנֶּה לִבּוֹ לְבַטָּלָה, הֲרֵי זֶה מִתְחַיֵּב בְּנַפְשׁוֹ.

ו. רַבִּי נְחוּנְיָא בֶּן הַקָּנָה אוֹמֵר: כָּל הַמְקַבֵּל עָלָיו עֹל תּוֹרָה, מַעֲבִירִים מִמֶּנּוּ עֹל מַלְכוּת וְעֹל דֶּרֶךְ אֶרֶץ; וְכָל הַפּוֹרֵק מִמֶּנּוּ עֹל תּוֹרָה, נוֹתְנִים עָלָיו עֹל מַלְכוּת וְעֹל דֶּרֶךְ אֶרֶץ.

רבי חנינא בן תרדיון was the father of Beruriah, famous wife of Rabbi Meir. He was burned at the stake, after the defeat of Bar-Kokhba in 135, for his refusal to obey the decrees of Hadrian.

שכינה ("habitation") denotes God's presence on earth. It is used as one of God's names.

2.   Rabbi Ḥanina, the deputy high-priest, said: Pray for the welfare of the government, since were it not for the fear of it men would swallow each other alive.

3.   Rabbi Ḥananyah ben Teradyon said: If two sit together and no words of Torah are spoken between them, they are a session of scoffers, of whom it is said: "[A good man] does not sit in the company of scoffers."[1] But when two sit together and interchange words of the Torah, the *Shekhinah* abides between them, as it is said: "Then those who revered the Lord spoke to each other, and the Lord listened and heard, and in his presence a record was written of those who revere the Lord and respect his name."[2] Now, this verse refers to two persons; whence do we know that even if one person engages in the study of the Torah, the Holy One, blessed be he, determines his reward? It is said: "Though he sits alone in thoughtful meditation, yet he receives" [the reward].[3]

4.   Rabbi Simeon said: If three have eaten at a table and have held no conversation on Torah, it is as though they had eaten of sacrifices offered to the dead [idols], as it is said: "For all their tables are full of filth without the presence of God."[4] But if three have eaten at a table and have conversed on Torah, they are as though they had eaten from the table of God, as it is said: "He said to me: This is the table which is in the presence of the Lord."[5]

5.   Rabbi Ḥanina ben Ḥakinai said: He who is awake at night, or travels alone on the road, and turns his mind to idle thoughts, commits a deadly sin.

6.   Rabbi Neḥunya ben ha-Kanah said: Whoever takes upon himself the yoke of the Torah will be relieved from the yoke of the government and the yoke of worldly affairs [struggle for existence]; whoever divests himself of the yoke of the Torah will be burdened with the yoke of the government and the yoke of worldly affairs.

רבי שמעון בן יוחאי, one of the most brilliant students of Rabbi Akiba. Strongly anti-Roman, he was forced for a long time to remain in hiding after the defeat of Bar-Kokhba. He is the supposed author of the *Zohar*, the mystical commentary on the Pentateuch. According to tradition, he died at Meron, northwest of Safed, on *Lag b'Omer*.

רבי חנינא בן חכיני was a disciple of Rabbi Akiba.

רבי נחוניא בן הקנה was a contemporary of Rabban Yoḥanan ben Zakkai. He attributed his attainment of great age to his forgiving nature, generosity in money matters and respect for the feelings of others (Megillah 28a).

---

[1]*Psalm* 1:1. [2]*Malachi* 3:16. [3]*Lamentations* 3:28. [4]*Isaiah* 28:8. [5]*Ezekiel* 41:22.

ז. רַבִּי חֲלַפְתָּא בֶּן דּוֹסָא, אִישׁ כְּפַר חֲנַנְיָא, אוֹמֵר: עֲשָׂרָה
שֶׁיּוֹשְׁבִים וְעוֹסְקִים בַּתּוֹרָה, שְׁכִינָה שְׁרוּיָה בֵּינֵיהֶם, שֶׁנֶּאֱמַר:
אֱלֹהִים נִצָּב בַּעֲדַת אֵל. וּמִנַּיִן אֲפִילוּ חֲמִשָּׁה, שֶׁנֶּאֱמַר: וַאֲגֻדָּתוֹ
עַל אֶרֶץ יְסָדָהּ. וּמִנַּיִן אֲפִילוּ שְׁלֹשָׁה, שֶׁנֶּאֱמַר: בְּקֶרֶב אֱלֹהִים
יִשְׁפֹּט. וּמִנַּיִן אֲפִילוּ שְׁנַיִם, שֶׁנֶּאֱמַר: אָז נִדְבְּרוּ יִרְאֵי יְיָ אִישׁ אֶל
רֵעֵהוּ, וַיַּקְשֵׁב יְיָ וַיִּשְׁמָע. וּמִנַּיִן אֲפִילוּ אֶחָד, שֶׁנֶּאֱמַר: בְּכָל
הַמָּקוֹם אֲשֶׁר אַזְכִּיר אֶת שְׁמִי, אָבֹא אֵלֶיךָ וּבֵרַכְתִּיךָ.

ח. רַבִּי אֶלְעָזָר, אִישׁ בַּרְתּוֹתָא, אוֹמֵר: תֶּן־לוֹ מִשֶּׁלּוֹ,
שֶׁאַתָּה וְשֶׁלְּךָ שֶׁלּוֹ. וְכֵן בְּדָוִד הוּא אוֹמֵר: כִּי מִמְּךָ הַכֹּל, וּמִיָּדְךָ
נָתַנּוּ לָךְ.

ט. רַבִּי יַעֲקֹב אוֹמֵר: הַמְהַלֵּךְ בַּדֶּרֶךְ וְשׁוֹנֶה, וּמַפְסִיק
מִמִּשְׁנָתוֹ וְאוֹמֵר: מַה נָּאֶה אִילָן זֶה, מַה נָּאֶה נִיר זֶה, מַעֲלֶה
עָלָיו הַכָּתוּב כְּאִלּוּ מִתְחַיֵּב בְּנַפְשׁוֹ.

י. רַבִּי דוֹסְתַּאי בַּר יַנַּאי, מִשּׁוּם רַבִּי מֵאִיר, אוֹמֵר: כָּל הַשּׁוֹכֵחַ
דָּבָר אֶחָד מִמִּשְׁנָתוֹ, מַעֲלֶה עָלָיו הַכָּתוּב כְּאִלּוּ מִתְחַיֵּב בְּנַפְשׁוֹ,
שֶׁנֶּאֱמַר: רַק הִשָּׁמֶר־לְךָ וּשְׁמֹר נַפְשְׁךָ מְאֹד, פֶּן תִּשְׁכַּח אֶת
הַדְּבָרִים אֲשֶׁר רָאוּ עֵינֶיךָ. יָכוֹל, אֲפִילוּ תָּקְפָה עָלָיו מִשְׁנָתוֹ,
תַּלְמוּד לוֹמַר: וּפֶן יָסוּרוּ מִלְּבָבְךָ כֹּל יְמֵי חַיֶּיךָ; הָא, אֵינוֹ
מִתְחַיֵּב בְּנַפְשׁוֹ עַד שֶׁיֵּשֵׁב וִיסִירֵם מִלִּבּוֹ.

יא. רַבִּי חֲנִינָא בֶּן דּוֹסָא אוֹמֵר: כֹּל שֶׁיִּרְאַת חֶטְאוֹ קוֹדֶמֶת
לְחָכְמָתוֹ, חָכְמָתוֹ מִתְקַיֶּמֶת; וְכֹל שֶׁחָכְמָתוֹ קוֹדֶמֶת לְיִרְאַת
חֶטְאוֹ, אֵין חָכְמָתוֹ מִתְקַיֶּמֶת.

רבי חלפתא בן דוסא was a disciple of Rabbi Meir.

רבי אלעזר איש ברתותא was a contemporary of Rabbi Akiba.

רבי יעקב was one of the teachers of Rabbi Judah ha-Nasi.

רבי דוסתאי בר ינאי was an older contemporary of Rabbi Judah ha-Nasi.

רבי חנינא בן דוסא was a disciple of Rabban Yoḥanan ben Zakkai.

7. Rabbi Ḥalafta ben Dosa of Kfar Ḥananya said: When ten people sit together and occupy themselves with the Torah, the *Shekhinah* abides among them, as it is said: "God stands in the godly congregation."[1] Whence do we know that the same applies even to five? It is said: "He has founded his band upon the earth."[2] Whence do we know that the same applies even to three? It is said: "In the midst of the judges he judges."[3] Whence do we know that the same applies even to two? It is said: "Then those who revered the Lord spoke to each other, and the Lord listened and heard."[4] Whence do we know that the same applies even to one? It is said: "In every place where I have my name mentioned I will come to you and bless you."[5]

8. Rabbi Elazar of Bertotha said: Give to God of his own, for you and yours are his. The same thought was expressed by David, who said: "For all things come from thee, and we have given thee only what is thine."[6]

9. Rabbi Jacob said: He who travels on the road while reviewing what he has learnt, and interrupts his study and says: "How fine is that tree, how fair is that field!" Scripture regards him as if he committed a grave sin [study is more important than the admiration of nature].

10. Rabbi Dostai ben Yannai said in the name of Rabbi Meir: Whoever forgets anything of what he has learned, Scripture regards him as if he committed a grave sin, for it is said: "Only take care, and watch yourself well that you do not forget the things which your eyes saw." Now, one might suppose that this applies even to a person who has forgotten because his study proved too hard for him; it is therefore explicitly added: "Lest they be removed from your heart all the days of your life."[7] Thus, he incurs a grave sin only when he deliberately removes the lessons from his heart.

11. Rabbi Ḥanina ben Dosa said: Anyone whose fear of sin precedes his wisdom [whose moral conduct means more to him than his learning], his wisdom shall endure; anyone whose wisdom precedes his fear of sin, his wisdom shall not endure.

רבי יעקב was one of the teachers of Rabbi Judah ha-Nasi.

רבי דוסתאי בר ינאי was an older contemporary of Rabbi Judah ha-Nasi.

רבי חנינא בן דוסא was a disciple of Rabban Yoḥanan ben Zakkai.

אין חכמתו מתקיימת Not being governed by the moral demands of wisdom, he will give up wisdom so that it might not trouble his conscience.

---

[1]*Psalm* 82:1.   [2]*Amos* 9:6.   [3]*Psalm* 82:1.   [4]*Malachi* 3:16.   [5]*Exodus* 20:24.
[6]I *Chronicles* 29:14.   [7]*Deuteronomy* 4:9.

יב. הוּא הָיָה אוֹמֵר: כֹּל שֶׁמַּעֲשָׂיו מְרֻבִּים מֵחָכְמָתוֹ,
חָכְמָתוֹ מִתְקַיֶּמֶת; וְכֹל שֶׁחָכְמָתוֹ מְרֻבָּה מִמַּעֲשָׂיו, אֵין חָכְמָתוֹ
מִתְקַיֶּמֶת.

יג. הוּא הָיָה אוֹמֵר: כֹּל שֶׁרוּחַ הַבְּרִיּוֹת נוֹחָה הֵימֶנּוּ, רוּחַ
הַמָּקוֹם נוֹחָה הֵימֶנּוּ; וְכֹל שֶׁאֵין רוּחַ הַבְּרִיּוֹת נוֹחָה הֵימֶנּוּ, אֵין
רוּחַ הַמָּקוֹם נוֹחָה הֵימֶנּוּ.

יד. רַבִּי דוֹסָא בֶּן הָרְכִּינַס אוֹמֵר: שֵׁנָה שֶׁל שַׁחֲרִית וְיַיִן שֶׁל
צָהֳרַיִם, וְשִׂיחַת הַיְלָדִים וִישִׁיבַת בָּתֵּי כְנֵסִיּוֹת שֶׁל עַמֵּי הָאָרֶץ,
מוֹצִיאִים אֶת הָאָדָם מִן הָעוֹלָם.

טו. רַבִּי אֶלְעָזָר הַמּוֹדָעִי אוֹמֵר: הַמְחַלֵּל אֶת הַקֳּדָשִׁים,
וְהַמְבַזֶּה אֶת הַמּוֹעֲדוֹת, וְהַמַּלְבִּין פְּנֵי חֲבֵרוֹ בָּרַבִּים, וְהַמֵּפֵר
בְּרִיתוֹ שֶׁל אַבְרָהָם אָבִינוּ, וְהַמְגַלֶּה פָנִים בַּתּוֹרָה שֶׁלֹּא
כַהֲלָכָה, אַף עַל פִּי שֶׁיֵּשׁ בְּיָדוֹ תּוֹרָה וּמַעֲשִׂים טוֹבִים, אֵין לוֹ
חֵלֶק לָעוֹלָם הַבָּא.

טז. רַבִּי יִשְׁמָעֵאל אוֹמֵר: הֱוֵי קַל לְרֹאשׁ וְנוֹחַ לְתִשְׁחֹרֶת,
וֶהֱוֵי מְקַבֵּל אֶת כָּל הָאָדָם בְּשִׂמְחָה.

יז. רַבִּי עֲקִיבָא אוֹמֵר: שְׂחוֹק וְקַלּוּת רֹאשׁ מַרְגִּילִים אֶת
הָאָדָם לְעֶרְוָה. מַסֹּרֶת סְיָג לַתּוֹרָה, מַעַשְׂרוֹת סְיָג לָעשֶׁר,
נְדָרִים סְיָג לַפְּרִישׁוּת; סְיָג לַחָכְמָה שְׁתִיקָה.

רבי דוסא בן הרכינס, a man of wealth, was a contemporary of Rabban
Yoḥanan ben Zakkai.

רבי אלעזר המודעי was killed by Bar-Kokhba who suspected him of being
in communication with the enemy during the siege of Bethar.

מגלה פנים בתורה.... one who interprets the Torah in contrast to the
authoritative rulings. It has been suggested that this phrase refers to the
allegorizers who accepted only the symbolic sense of the commandments and
rejected the traditional interpretation.

12. He used to say: Anyone whose deeds exceed his wisdom, his wisdom shall endure; anyone whose wisdom exceeds his deeds, his wisdom shall not endure.

13. He used to say: Anyone who is liked by his fellow men is liked by God; anyone who is not liked by his fellow men is not liked by God.

14. Rabbi Dosa ben Horkinas said: Morning sleep [late sleeping], wine drinking at noon, [frivolous] childish talk, and attending the meeting-places of the ignorant shorten a man's life.

15. Rabbi Elazar of Modin said: He who profanes sacred objects, slights the festivals, puts his fellow man to shame in public, breaks the covenant of our father Abraham, or misinterprets the Torah—even though he has Torah and good deeds to his credit—has no share in the world to come.

16. Rabbi Ishmael said: Be submissive to a superior and kindly to the young; and receive all men cheerfully.

17. Rabbi Akiba said: Jesting and light-headedness lead a man on to lewdness. The *Massorah* [the tradition as to the correct text of the Scriptures] is a fence to the Torah [and preserves its integrity]; tithes form a fence to wealth; vows are a fence [a help] to self-restraint; a fence to wisdom is silence.

רבי ישמעאל, when a boy, was taken prisoner to Rome after the fall of Jerusalem, and was ransomed by Rabbi Joshua ben Ḥananyah. He formulated the "thirteen rules" by which the Torah is to be interpreted. During the Hadrianic persecutions he died as a martyr.

תשחורת has been variously rendered. It is here rendered in the sense of "youth" on the basis of שחרות in Ecclesiastes 11:10.

רבי עקיבא, one of the most important interpreters of oral tradition, began his career as a student at the age of forty. He soon became one of the most prominent leaders of Palestine, and trained a vast number of students in his academy at Bné Brak, east of Jaffa. He is the hero of many stories which are tributes to his unselfishness, loyalty and devotion. One of the main supporters of Bar-Kokhba, he died as a martyr in 135.

מעשרות סיג לעושר that is, contributions to charity protect the donor from spending his fortune wastefully. This is generally illustrated by the proverbial saying: עשר בשביל שתתעשר "Give tithes so that you will become rich," a play on the words עשר תעשר (Deuteronomy 14:22).

יח. הוּא הָיָה אוֹמֵר: חָבִיב אָדָם, שֶׁנִּבְרָא בְצֶלֶם; חִבָּה
יְתֵרָה נוֹדַעַת לוֹ שֶׁנִּבְרָא בְצֶלֶם, שֶׁנֶּאֱמַר: כִּי בְּצֶלֶם אֱלֹהִים
עָשָׂה אֶת הָאָדָם. חֲבִיבִים יִשְׂרָאֵל, שֶׁנִּקְרְאוּ בָנִים לַמָּקוֹם;
חִבָּה יְתֵרָה נוֹדַעַת לָהֶם שֶׁנִּקְרְאוּ בָנִים לַמָּקוֹם, שֶׁנֶּאֱמַר: בָּנִים
אַתֶּם לַיְיָ אֱלֹהֵיכֶם. חֲבִיבִים יִשְׂרָאֵל, שֶׁנִּתַּן לָהֶם כְּלִי חֶמְדָּה;
חִבָּה יְתֵרָה נוֹדַעַת לָהֶם שֶׁנִּתַּן לָהֶם כְּלִי חֶמְדָּה, שֶׁבּוֹ נִבְרָא
הָעוֹלָם, שֶׁנֶּאֱמַר: כִּי לֶקַח טוֹב נָתַתִּי לָכֶם, תּוֹרָתִי אַל תַּעֲזֹבוּ.

יט. הַכֹּל צָפוּי, וְהָרְשׁוּת נְתוּנָה, וּבְטוֹב הָעוֹלָם נָדוֹן, וְהַכֹּל
לְפִי רֹב הַמַּעֲשֶׂה.

כ. הוּא הָיָה אוֹמֵר: הַכֹּל נָתוּן בָּעֵרָבוֹן, וּמְצוּדָה פְרוּשָׂה
עַל כָּל הַחַיִּים. הֶחָנוּת פְּתוּחָה, וְהַחֶנְוָנִי מַקִּיף, וְהַפִּנְקָס פָּתוּחַ,
וְהַיָּד כּוֹתֶבֶת, וְכָל הָרוֹצֶה לִלְווֹת יָבֹא וְיִלְוֶה; וְהַגַּבָּאִים
מְחַזְּרִים תָּדִיר בְּכָל יוֹם וְנִפְרָעִים מִן הָאָדָם, מִדַּעְתּוֹ וְשֶׁלֹּא
מִדַּעְתּוֹ, וְיֵשׁ לָהֶם עַל מַה שֶׁיִּסְמֹכוּ. וְהַדִּין דִּין אֱמֶת, וְהַכֹּל
מְתֻקָּן לִסְעֻדָּה.

כא. רַבִּי אֶלְעָזָר בֶּן עֲזַרְיָה אוֹמֵר: אִם אֵין תּוֹרָה, אֵין
דֶּרֶךְ אֶרֶץ; אִם אֵין דֶּרֶךְ אֶרֶץ, אֵין תּוֹרָה. אִם אֵין חָכְמָה, אֵין
יִרְאָה; אִם אֵין יִרְאָה, אֵין חָכְמָה. אִם אֵין דַּעַת, אֵין בִּינָה; אִם
אֵין בִּינָה, אֵין דַּעַת. אִם אֵין קֶמַח, אֵין תּוֹרָה; אִם אֵין תּוֹרָה,
אֵין קֶמַח.

הרשות נתונה that is, God's foreknowledge does not predetermine man's actions, good or bad. In matters of ethical conduct man has the ability to choose between alternative possibilities of action.

הכל לפי רוב המעשה Man's good deeds are set off against his evil deeds, and he is condemned or acquitted according to the preponderance of his good or bad deeds.

הכל נתון בערבון is a saying which employs the language of everyday business life to drive home the thought with greater force.

18. He used to say: Beloved is man, for he was created in the image of God; it is by special divine love that he is informed that he was created in the image of God, as it is said: "For God made man in his own image."[1] Beloved are Israel, for they were called the children of God; it is by special divine love that they are informed that they were called the children of God, as it is said: "You are the children of the Lord your God."[2] Beloved are Israel, for to them was given a precious instrument [the Torah]; it is by special divine love that they are informed that to them was given the precious instrument through which the world was created, as it is said: "For I give you good doctrine; forsake not my Torah."[3]

19. Everything is foreseen [by God], yet freewill is granted [to man]; the world is ruled with divine goodness, yet all is according to the amount of man's work.

20. He used to say: Everything is given on pledge, and a net is spread for all the living [none can escape divine justice]; the store is open, and the storekeeper [God] allows credit; the ledger is open, and the hand writes; whoever wishes to borrow may come and borrow, but the collectors go around regularly every day and exact payment from man, whether or not he realizes [that he is punished for his sins]; they have good authority on which they can rely, since the judgment is just; and all is prepared for the banquet [the reward of the righteous is assured].

21. Rabbi Elazar ben Azaryah said: Where there is no Torah, there is no proper conduct; where there is no proper conduct, there is no Torah. Where there is no wisdom, there is no reverence; where there is no reverence, there is no wisdom. Where there is no knowledge, there is no understanding; where there is no understanding, there is no knowledge. Where there is no bread, there is no Torah; where there is no Torah, there is no bread.

רבי אלעזר בן עזריה was elected president of the Sanhedrin when Rabban Gamaliel II was temporarily deposed. When Rabban Gamaliel was restored to his former position, Rabbi Elazar was retained as vice-president of the Sanhedrin. He used his great wealth for the welfare of his people during the Roman persecutions before the revolt of Bar-Kokhba.

---

[1] *Genesis* 9:6. [2] *Deuteronomy* 14:1. [3] *Proverbs* 4:2.

כב: הוּא הָיָה אוֹמֵר: כֹּל שֶׁחָכְמָתוֹ מְרֻבָּה מִמַּעֲשָׂיו, לְמָה הוּא דוֹמֶה, לְאִילָן שֶׁעֲנָפָיו מְרֻבִּים וְשָׁרָשָׁיו מֻעָטִים, וְהָרוּחַ בָּאָה וְעוֹקַרְתּוֹ וְהוֹפַכְתּוֹ עַל פָּנָיו, שֶׁנֶּאֱמַר: וְהָיָה כְּעַרְעָר בָּעֲרָבָה, וְלֹא יִרְאֶה כִּי יָבוֹא טוֹב, וְשָׁכַן חֲרֵרִים בַּמִּדְבָּר, אֶרֶץ מְלֵחָה וְלֹא תֵשֵׁב. אֲבָל כָּל שֶׁמַּעֲשָׂיו מְרֻבִּים מֵחָכְמָתוֹ, לְמָה הוּא דוֹמֶה, לְאִילָן שֶׁעֲנָפָיו מֻעָטִים וְשָׁרָשָׁיו מְרֻבִּים, שֶׁאֲפִלוּ כָּל הָרוּחוֹת שֶׁבָּעוֹלָם בָּאוֹת וְנוֹשְׁבוֹת בּוֹ, אֵין מְזִיזִים אוֹתוֹ מִמְּקוֹמוֹ, שֶׁנֶּאֱמַר: וְהָיָה כְּעֵץ שָׁתוּל עַל מַיִם, וְעַל יוּבַל יְשַׁלַּח שָׁרָשָׁיו, וְלֹא יִרְאֶה כִּי יָבֹא חֹם, וְהָיָה עָלֵהוּ רַעֲנָן, וּבִשְׁנַת בַּצֹּרֶת לֹא יִדְאָג, וְלֹא יָמִישׁ מֵעֲשׂוֹת פֶּרִי.

כג: רַבִּי אֶלְעָזָר בֶּן חִסְמָא אוֹמֵר: קִנִּין וּפִתְחֵי נִדָּה הֵן הֵן גּוּפֵי הֲלָכוֹת; תְּקוּפוֹת וְגֵמַטְרִיָּאוֹת פַּרְפְּרָאוֹת לַחָכְמָה.

רַבִּי חֲנַנְיָא בֶּן עֲקַשְׁיָא אוֹמֵר: רָצָה הַקָּדוֹשׁ בָּרוּךְ הוּא לְזַכּוֹת אֶת יִשְׂרָאֵל, לְפִיכָךְ הִרְבָּה לָהֶם תּוֹרָה וּמִצְוֹת, שֶׁנֶּאֱמַר: יְיָ חָפֵץ לְמַעַן צִדְקוֹ, יַגְדִּיל תּוֹרָה וְיַאְדִּיר.

פֶּרֶק רְבִיעִי

כָּל יִשְׂרָאֵל יֵשׁ לָהֶם חֵלֶק לָעוֹלָם הַבָּא, שֶׁנֶּאֱמַר: וְעַמֵּךְ כֻּלָּם צַדִּיקִים, לְעוֹלָם יִירְשׁוּ אָרֶץ; נֵצֶר מַטָּעַי, מַעֲשֵׂה יָדַי לְהִתְפָּאֵר.

כל שחכמתו מרובה.... is an elaboration of the maxim expressed above (3:12) by Rabbi Ḥanina ben Dosa. Moral goodness is more essential than speculative thought. Wisdom is valueless unless it improves a man's character. If he has more theoretical knowledge than good deeds, his life is ruined by his failure to live up to his ethical principles. On the other hand, a good life is possible even if it is not based on much learning.

22. He used to say: One whose wisdom exceeds his deeds, to what is he like? To a tree that has many branches and few roots, so that when the wind comes, it plucks it up and turns it over, as it is said: "And he shall be like a lonely tree in the desert, and shall not see the coming of good; he shall inhabit the parched places in the wilderness, a salt land and uninhabited."[1] But one whose deeds exceed his wisdom, to what is he like? To a tree that has few branches and many roots, so that even if all the winds in the world come and blow upon it, they cannot move it out of its place, as it is said: "And he shall be like a tree planted by waters, that spreads out its roots beside a stream; it sees not the coming of heat, and its leaves are ever green; in a year of drought it is not troubled, and ceases not to bear fruit."[2]

23. Rabbi Elazar Ḥisma said: The laws concerning the sacrifices of birds and the purification of women are essential precepts; astronomy and geometry are the auxiliaries of wisdom.

Rabbi Ḥananyah ben Akashyah said: The Holy One, blessed be he, desired to purify Israel; hence he gave them a Torah rich in rules of conduct, as it is said: "The Lord was pleased, for the sake of [Israel's] righteousness, to render the Torah great and glorious."[3]

CHAPTER FOUR

All Israel have a share in the world to come, as it is said; "Your people shall all be righteous; they shall possess the land forever; they are a plant of my own, the work of my hands, wherein I may glory."[4]

רבי אלעזר חסמא, a disciple of Rabbi Akiba, was famous for his knowledge of astronomy and physics. He means to say that though the laws concerning bird sacrifices do not apply when the Temple no longer exists, and though certain laws seem unattractive as a subject of study, they are nevertheless of highest importance, because they form the precepts of the Torah. The primary meaning of פרפרת is dessert, appetizer. Some derive this word from the Greek in the sense of periphery, outer circle, as opposed to the essence of the Torah. According to this view, Rabbi Elazar means to say that astronomy and geometry are of secondary importance to the study of the Torah.

---

[1] *Jeremiah* 17:6.　[2] *Jeremiah* 17:8.　[3] *Isaiah* 42:21.　[4] *Isaiah* 60:21.

א. בֶּן זוֹמָא אוֹמֵר: אֵיזֶהוּ חָכָם, הַלּוֹמֵד מִכָּל אָדָם,
שֶׁנֶּאֱמַר: מִכָּל מְלַמְּדַי הִשְׂכַּלְתִּי (כִּי עֵדְוֹתֶיךָ שִׂיחָה לִי). אֵיזֶהוּ
גִבּוֹר, הַכּוֹבֵשׁ אֶת יִצְרוֹ, שֶׁנֶּאֱמַר: טוֹב אֶרֶךְ אַפַּיִם מִגִּבּוֹר,
וּמוֹשֵׁל בְּרוּחוֹ מִלֹּכֵד עִיר. אֵיזֶהוּ עָשִׁיר, הַשָּׂמֵחַ בְּחֶלְקוֹ,
שֶׁנֶּאֱמַר: יְגִיעַ כַּפֶּיךָ כִּי תֹאכֵל, אַשְׁרֶיךָ וְטוֹב לָךְ. אַשְׁרֶיךָ,
בָּעוֹלָם הַזֶּה; וְטוֹב לָךְ, לָעוֹלָם הַבָּא. אֵיזֶהוּ מְכֻבָּד, הַמְכַבֵּד
אֶת הַבְּרִיּוֹת, שֶׁנֶּאֱמַר: כִּי מְכַבְּדַי אֲכַבֵּד, וּבֹזַי יֵקָלּוּ.

ב. בֶּן עַזַּי אוֹמֵר: הֱוֵי רָץ לְמִצְוָה קַלָּה (כְּלַחֲמוּרָה) וּבוֹרֵחַ
מִן הָעֲבֵרָה, שֶׁמִּצְוָה גּוֹרֶרֶת מִצְוָה, וַעֲבֵרָה גּוֹרֶרֶת עֲבֵרָה;
שֶׁשְּׂכַר מִצְוָה מִצְוָה, וּשְׂכַר עֲבֵרָה עֲבֵרָה.

ג. הוּא הָיָה אוֹמֵר: אַל תְּהִי בָז לְכָל אָדָם, וְאַל תְּהִי מַפְלִיג
לְכָל דָּבָר, שֶׁאֵין לְךָ אָדָם שֶׁאֵין לוֹ שָׁעָה, וְאֵין לְךָ דָּבָר שֶׁאֵין
לוֹ מָקוֹם.

ד. רַבִּי לְוִיטַס, אִישׁ יַבְנֶה, אוֹמֵר: מְאֹד מְאֹד הֱוֵי שְׁפַל
רוּחַ, שֶׁתִּקְוַת אֱנוֹשׁ רִמָּה.

ה. רַבִּי יוֹחָנָן בֶּן בְּרוֹקָא אוֹמֵר: כָּל הַמְחַלֵּל שֵׁם שָׁמַיִם
בַּסֵּתֶר, נִפְרָעִים מִמֶּנּוּ בַּגָּלוּי. אֶחָד שׁוֹגֵג וְאֶחָד מֵזִיד בְּחִלּוּל
הַשֵּׁם

ו. רַבִּי יִשְׁמָעֵאל בְּנוֹ אוֹמֵר: הַלּוֹמֵד עַל מְנָת לְלַמֵּד,
מַסְפִּיקִים בְּיָדוֹ לִלְמֹד וּלְלַמֵּד; וְהַלּוֹמֵד עַל מְנָת לַעֲשׂוֹת,
מַסְפִּיקִים בְּיָדוֹ לִלְמֹד וּלְלַמֵּד, לִשְׁמֹר וְלַעֲשׂוֹת.

שמעון בן זומא, a younger contemporary of Rabbi Akiba, was a colleague of
שמעון בן עזי (quoted in the next paragraph). Their own names are omitted
because they both died at an early age, before they could be ordained. They
were deeply interested in mysticism and theosophy.

מצוה an act performed in the interests of religion or of fellow men.

· **שכר מצוה מצוה** Habits are formed by the repetition of single acts.

1. Ben Zoma said: Who is wise? He who learns from every man, as it is said: "From all my teachers I gained wisdom."[1] Who is strong? He who subdues his [evil] impulse, as it is said: "He who is slow to anger is better than a strong man; he who rules his spirit is better than one who conquers a city."[2] Who is rich? He who is content with his lot, as it is said: "When you eat of the toil of your hands, happy shall you be, and it shall be well with you."[3] *Happy shall you be* in this world; *and it shall be well with you* in the world to come. Who is honored? He who honors his fellowmen, as it is said: "Those who honor me [by honoring man, created in the image of God] I will honor, and those who despise me shall be lightly esteemed."[4]

2. Ben Azzai said: Run to perform even a minor *mitzvah*, and flee from transgression; for one good deed draws [in its train] another good deed, and one transgression leads to another; for the reward of a good deed is a good deed, and the reward of sin is sin [virtue is its own reward, and sin its own penalty].

3. He used to say: Do not despise any man, and do not consider anything as impossible; for there is not a man who has not his hour, and there is not a thing that has not its place.

4. Rabbi Levitas of Yavneh said: Be exceedingly humble, since the end of man is worms.

5. Rabbi Yoḥanan ben Berokah said: Whoever profanes the name of God secretly is punished publicly, whether the profanation is committed intentionally or unintentionally.

6. Rabbi Ishmael said: He who learns in order to teach will be granted adequate means to learn and to teach; but he who learns in order to practise will be granted adequate means to learn and to teach, to observe and to practise.

רבי לויטס was a contemporary of Rabbi Akiba.

תקוה limit, end; compare הנותן תקוה לנזירותו, ("he who sets a limit to . . .") and the phrase אחריתנו רמה in the *nei'lah* service.

רבי יוחנן בן ברוקא was a disciple of Rabbi Joshua ben Ḥananyah (second century).

חלול השם ("defamation of God's name") is an act performed in defiance of religious or ethical principles.

רבי ישמעאל Some texts add בנו ("his son").

---

[1] *Psalm* 119:99.   [2] *Proverbs* 16:32.   [3] *Psalm* 128:2.   [4] *I Samuel* 2:30.

ז. רַבִּי צָדוֹק אוֹמֵר: אַל תִּפְרוֹשׁ מִן הַצִּבּוּר, וְאַל תַּעַשׂ עַצְמְךָ כְּעוֹרְכֵי הַדַּיָּנִים, וְאַל תַּעֲשֶׂהָ עֲטָרָה לְהִתְגַּדֶּל־בָּהּ, וְלֹא קַרְדֹּם לַחְפָּר־בָּהּ. וְכָךְ הָיָה הִלֵּל אוֹמֵר: וּדְאִשְׁתַּמַּשׁ בְּתַגָּא חֲלָף. הָא לָמַדְתָּ, כָּל הַנֶּהֱנֶה מִדִּבְרֵי תוֹרָה נוֹטֵל חַיָּיו מִן הָעוֹלָם.

ח. רַבִּי יוֹסֵי אוֹמֵר: כָּל הַמְכַבֵּד אֶת הַתּוֹרָה, גּוּפוֹ מְכֻבָּד עַל הַבְּרִיּוֹת; וְכָל הַמְחַלֵּל אֶת הַתּוֹרָה, גּוּפוֹ מְחֻלָּל עַל הַבְּרִיּוֹת.

ט. רַבִּי יִשְׁמָעֵאל בְּנוֹ אוֹמֵר: הַחוֹשֵׂךְ עַצְמוֹ מִן הַדִּין, פּוֹרֵק מִמֶּנּוּ אֵיבָה וְגָזֵל וּשְׁבוּעַת שָׁוְא; וְהַגַּס לִבּוֹ בְּהוֹרָאָה שׁוֹטֶה, רָשָׁע וְגַס רוּחַ.

י. הוּא הָיָה אוֹמֵר: אַל תְּהִי דָן יְחִידִי, שֶׁאֵין דָּן יְחִידִי אֶלָּא אֶחָד; וְאַל תֹּאמַר קַבְּלוּ דַעְתִּי, שֶׁהֵם רַשָּׁאִים וְלֹא אָתָּה.

יא. רַבִּי יוֹנָתָן אוֹמֵר: כָּל הַמְקַיֵּם אֶת הַתּוֹרָה מֵעֹנִי, סוֹפוֹ לְקַיְּמָהּ מֵעֹשֶׁר; וְכָל הַמְבַטֵּל אֶת הַתּוֹרָה מֵעֹשֶׁר, סוֹפוֹ לְבַטְּלָהּ מֵעֹנִי.

יב. רַבִּי מֵאִיר אוֹמֵר: הֱוֵי מְמַעֵט בְּעֵסֶק וַעֲסֹק בַּתּוֹרָה, וֶהֱוֵי שְׁפַל רוּחַ בִּפְנֵי כָל אָדָם. וְאִם בָּטַלְתָּ מִן הַתּוֹרָה, יֶשׁ־לְךָ בְטֵלִים הַרְבֵּה כְּנֶגְדֶּךָ; וְאִם עָמַלְתָּ בַתּוֹרָה, יֶשׁ־לוֹ שָׂכָר הַרְבֵּה לִתֶּן־לָךְ.

רבי צדוק was probably the one who is said to have fasted for forty years, praying that Jerusalem should not be destroyed.

יוסי בן חלפתא, one of the most distinguished disciples of Rabbi Akiba, compiled the chronological treatise *Seder Olam* ("Order of the World"), from the creation until the revolt of Bar-Kokhba.

רבי ישמעאל בנו Some texts omit בנו ("his son").

הגס לבו בהוראה one who is too sure of himself, not realizing that the judicial position is one that involves infinite pains in the sifting of evidence and in reaching a decision.

7. Rabbi Zadok said: Do not keep aloof from the community; do not [as a judge] play the part of a counselor; do not make of the Torah a crown wherewith to magnify yourself, nor a spade wherewith to dig. Hillel used to say: "He who makes unworthy use of the crown [of the Torah] shall perish." Hence, whoever makes selfish use of the Torah takes his own life.

8. Rabbi Yosé said: Whoever honors the Torah will himself be honored by men; whoever dishonors the Torah will himself be dishonored by men.

9. Rabbi Ishmael his son said: He who avoids entering into litigation [and seeks a friendly settlement] rids himself of hatred, robbery and perjury; he who proudly lays down decisions is foolish, wicked and arrogant.

10. He used to say: Do not judge alone, for none may judge alone except One [God]; do not say [to your co-judges]: "Accept my view," for they [who are in the majority] are entitled to say that, but not you.

11. Rabbi Jonathan said: Whoever fulfills the Torah despite poverty shall in the end fulfill it in the midst of wealth; whoever neglects the Torah in the midst of wealth shall in the end neglect it on account of poverty.

12. Rabbi Meir said: Do rather less business and occupy yourself with the Torah; be humble before all men; if you neglect the Torah, you will have many disturbing causes in your way; but if you toil in the Torah, God has abundant reward to give you.

רבי יונתן was a disciple of Rabbi Akiba.

רבי מאיר, the greatest of Rabbi Akiba's disciples, was called *Meir* ("enlightener") on account of his pre-eminence as a teacher and lecturer. His wife, Beruriah, was herself a scholar, whose wise utterances and legal views are quoted in the Talmud. By profession a scribe, whose Bible copies were given special notice, he denounced those who acquire learning but fail to impart it to others. In order to obtain knowledge from all possible sources, he cultivated the friendship of Elisha ben Abuyah (אחר), who had turned heretic. He departed from Palestine, and died in Asia Minor. His last wish was: "Bury me by the seashore, that the waves which wash my fatherland may wash also my bones." His name occurs some 800 times in tannaitic literature.

יג. רַבִּי אֱלִיעֶזֶר בֶּן יַעֲקֹב אוֹמֵר: הָעוֹשֶׂה מִצְוָה אַחַת קוֹנֶה
לוֹ פְּרַקְלִיט אֶחָד, וְהָעוֹבֵר עֲבֵרָה אַחַת קוֹנֶה לוֹ קַטֵּגוֹר אֶחָד.
תְּשׁוּבָה וּמַעֲשִׂים טוֹבִים כִּתְרִיס בִּפְנֵי הַפֻּרְעָנוּת.

יד. רַבִּי יוֹחָנָן הַסַּנְדְּלָר אוֹמֵר: כָּל כְּנֵסִיָּה שֶׁהִיא לְשֵׁם
שָׁמַיִם, סוֹפָהּ לְהִתְקַיֵּם; וְשֶׁאֵינָהּ לְשֵׁם שָׁמַיִם, אֵין סוֹפָהּ
לְהִתְקַיֵּם.

טו. רַבִּי אֶלְעָזָר בֶּן שַׁמּוּעַ אוֹמֵר: יְהִי כְבוֹד תַּלְמִידְךָ
חָבִיב עָלֶיךָ כְּשֶׁלָּךְ, וּכְבוֹד חֲבֵרְךָ כְּמוֹרָא רַבָּךְ, וּמוֹרָא רַבְּךָ
כְּמוֹרָא שָׁמָיִם.

טז. רַבִּי יְהוּדָה אוֹמֵר: הֱוֵי זָהִיר בְּתַלְמוּד, שֶׁשִּׁגְגַת תַּלְמוּד
עוֹלָה זָדוֹן.

יז. רַבִּי שִׁמְעוֹן אוֹמֵר: שְׁלֹשָׁה כְתָרִים הֵן: כֶּתֶר תּוֹרָה,
וְכֶתֶר כְּהֻנָּה, וְכֶתֶר מַלְכוּת; וְכֶתֶר שֵׁם טוֹב עוֹלֶה עַל גַּבֵּיהֶן.

יח. רַבִּי נְהוֹרַי אוֹמֵר: הֱוֵי גוֹלֶה לִמְקוֹם תּוֹרָה, וְאַל תֹּאמַר
שֶׁהִיא תָבוֹא אַחֲרֶיךָ, שֶׁחֲבֵרֶיךָ יְקַיְּמוּהָ בְּיָדֶךָ, וְאֶל בִּינָתְךָ
אַל תִּשָּׁעֵן.

יט. רַבִּי יַנַּי אוֹמֵר: אֵין בְּיָדֵינוּ לֹא מִשַּׁלְוַת הָרְשָׁעִים, וְאַף
לֹא מִיִּסּוּרֵי הַצַּדִּיקִים.

כ. רַבִּי מַתְּתְיָה בֶּן חָרָשׁ אוֹמֵר: הֱוֵי מַקְדִּים בִּשְׁלוֹם כָּל
אָדָם, וֶהֱוֵי זָנָב לָאֲרָיוֹת וְאַל תְּהִי רֹאשׁ לַשְׁעָלִים.

רבי אליעזר בן יעקב, and the *Tannaim* who are quoted in paragraphs 13–18, lived in the second century and studied under the guidance of Rabbi Akiba.

קונה לו פרקליט is to be compared with the midrashic statement: "If a man performs one *mitzvah*, God gives him one angel to guard him. . . If he performs two *mitzvoth*, God gives him two angels to guard him. . ." (*Shemoth Rabbah*, 32). Each good deed pleads for the man who stands in judgment before God.

תשבה ומעשים טובים is frequently emphasized in talmudic literature. One of the rabbis was in the habit of saying: "The chief purpose of wisdom is

13.   Rabbi Eliezer ben Jacob said: He who performs one *mitzvah* gains for himself one advocate; he who commits one transgression acquires for himself one accuser. Repentance and good deeds are as a shield against punishment.

14.   Rabbi Yoḥanan ha-Sandlar said: Any assembly which is for the sake of Heaven [for the promotion of a noble purpose] will be of permanent value, but one which is not for the sake of Heaven will not be of permanent value.

15.   Rabbi Elazar ben Shammua said: Let the honor of your student be as dear to you as your own, and the honor of your colleague be like the reverence due to your teacher, and the reverence for your teacher be like the reverence for Heaven.

16.   Rabbi Judah said: Be careful in teaching, for an error in teaching amounts to intentional sin.

17.   Rabbi Simeon said: There are three crowns: the crown of Torah, the crown of priesthood, and the crown of royalty; but the crown of a good name excels them all.

18.   Rabbi Nehorai said: Go as a voluntary exile to a place of Torah, and do not say that the Torah will seek after you, for it is your fellow students who will make it your permanent possession; and do not rely on your own understanding.

19.   Rabbi Yannai said: It is not in our power to explain why the wicked are at ease, or why the righteous suffer.

20.   Rabbi Mattithyah ben Ḥeresh said: Meet every man with a friendly greeting; be the tail among lions rather than the head among foxes.

---

repentance and good deeds; let no man who engages in learning treat his parents with contempt. . ." (Berakhoth 17a).

רבי יוחנן הסנדלר was an Alexandrian. His surname is due either to his occupation as a sandal-maker, or to the fact that he was a native of Alexandria.

שגגת תלמוד עולה זדון if the error is due to carelessness.

רבי נהוראי is identified with Rabbi Elazar ben Arakh and Rabbi Meir.

חבריך יקיימוה בידך Torah knowledge is acquired by association with scholars. ·

אל בינתך אל תשען a quotation from Proverbs 3:5.

רבי ינאי is not mentioned elsewhere in tannaitic literature.

רבי מתתיה lived in Rome in the middle of the second century.

כא. רַבִּי יַעֲקֹב אוֹמֵר: הָעוֹלָם הַזֶּה דּוֹמֶה לִפְרוֹזְדוֹר בִּפְנֵי הָעוֹלָם הַבָּא; הַתְקֵן עַצְמְךָ בַּפְּרוֹזְדוֹר, כְּדֵי שֶׁתִּכָּנֵס לַטְּרַקְלִין.

כב. הוּא הָיָה אוֹמֵר: יָפָה שָׁעָה אַחַת בִּתְשׁוּבָה וּמַעֲשִׂים טוֹבִים בָּעוֹלָם הַזֶּה מִכָּל חַיֵּי הָעוֹלָם הַבָּא; וְיָפָה שָׁעָה אַחַת שֶׁל קֹרַת רוּחַ בָּעוֹלָם הַבָּא מִכָּל חַיֵּי הָעוֹלָם הַזֶּה.

כג. רַבִּי שִׁמְעוֹן בֶּן אֶלְעָזָר אוֹמֵר: אַל תְּרַצֶּה אֶת חֲבֵרְךָ בִּשְׁעַת כַּעֲסוֹ, וְאַל תְּנַחֲמֵהוּ בְּשָׁעָה שֶׁמֵּתוֹ מֻטָּל לְפָנָיו, וְאַל תִּשְׁאַל לוֹ בִּשְׁעַת נִדְרוֹ, וְאַל תִּשְׁתַּדֵּל לִרְאוֹתוֹ בִּשְׁעַת קַלְקָלָתוֹ.

כד. שְׁמוּאֵל הַקָּטָן אוֹמֵר: בִּנְפֹל אוֹיִבְךָ אַל תִּשְׂמָח, וּבִכָּשְׁלוֹ אַל יָגֵל לִבֶּךָ, פֶּן יִרְאֶה יְיָ וְרַע בְּעֵינָיו, וְהֵשִׁיב מֵעָלָיו אַפּוֹ.

כה. אֱלִישָׁע בֶּן אֲבוּיָה אוֹמֵר: הַלּוֹמֵד יֶלֶד, לְמָה הוּא דוֹמֶה, לִדְיוֹ כְּתוּבָה עַל נְיָר חָדָשׁ; וְהַלּוֹמֵד זָקֵן, לְמָה הוּא דוֹמֶה, לִדְיוֹ כְּתוּבָה עַל נְיָר מָחוּק.

כו. רַבִּי יוֹסֵי בַּר יְהוּדָה, אִישׁ כְּפַר הַבַּבְלִי, אוֹמֵר: הַלּוֹמֵד מִן הַקְּטַנִּים, לְמָה הוּא דוֹמֶה, לְאוֹכֵל עֲנָבִים קֵהוֹת וְשׁוֹתֶה יַיִן מִגִּתּוֹ; וְהַלּוֹמֵד מִן הַזְּקֵנִים, לְמָה הוּא דוֹמֶה, לְאוֹכֵל עֲנָבִים בְּשׁוּלוֹת וְשׁוֹתֶה יַיִן יָשָׁן.

כז. רַבִּי מֵאִיר אוֹמֵר: אַל תִּסְתַּכֵּל בְּקַנְקַן אֶלָּא בְּמַה שֶּׁיֶּשׁ־ בּוֹ: יֵשׁ קַנְקַן חָדָשׁ מָלֵא יָשָׁן, וְיָשָׁן שֶׁאֲפִילוּ חָדָשׁ אֵין בּוֹ.

רבי שמעון בן אלעזר was a disciple of Rabbi Meir and lived during the second century.

אל תרצה את חברך ... a warning against unintended provocation.

שמואל הקטן lived towards the end of the first century, and was famous for his humility; hence the surname "ha-Katan." The saying reported in his name is a quotation from Proverbs 24:17-18. It has been suggested that the phrase שמואל הקטן אומר (=שה"א שהרי הכתוב אומר) is an amplification of the initials

21. Rabbi Jacob said: This world is like a vestibule before the world to come; prepare yourself in the vestibule, so that you may enter the banquet hall.

22. He used to say: One hour spent in repentance and good deeds in this world is better [more exhilarating] than the whole life of the world to come; yet one hour of satisfaction in the world to come is better than a whole life of this world.

23. Rabbi Simeon ben Elazar said: Do not pacify your fellow in the hour of his anger; do not comfort him while his dead lies before him; do not question him at the time he makes a vow; and do not try to see him in the hour of his disgrace.

24. Samuel ha-Katan said: "Rejoice not when your enemy falls, and let not your heart exult when he stumbles; lest the Lord see it and be displeased, and he divert his wrath from him [to you]."[1]

25. Elisha ben Avuyah said: If one learns when he is young, to what is it like? To ink written on new [clean] paper. If one learns when he is old, to what is it like? To ink written on blotted paper.

26. Rabbi Yosé ben Judah of Kfar ha-Bavli said: He who learns from the young, to what is he like? To one who eats unripe grapes, or drinks [new] wine from his vat. He who learns from the old, to what is he like? To one who eats ripe grapes, or drinks old wine.

27. Rabbi Meir said: Do not look at the flask but at what it contains: a new flask may be filled with old wine and an old flask may be empty even of new wine [a man's age is not a reliable index to his learning].

---

introducing biblical support of the preceding statement that one must not try to see anyone in disgrace.

אלישע בן אבויה, known as *Aḥer* ("the other"), lived in the second century as one of the great scholars of the period, a colleague of Rabbi Akiba and teacher of Rabbi Meir, but turned heretic under the influence of Greek philosophy and theosophic speculations. Whether he completely broke away from Judaism is a matter of doubt.

רבי יוסי בר יהודה was an older contemporary of Rabbi Judah ha-Nasi (towards the end of the second century). *Kfar ha-Bavli* was a village in Galilee.

---

[1] *Proverbs* 24:17-18.

כח. רַבִּי אֶלְעָזָר הַקַּפָּר אוֹמֵר: הַקִּנְאָה וְהַתַּאֲוָה וְהַכָּבוֹד מוֹצִיאִים אֶת הָאָדָם מִן הָעוֹלָם.

כט. הוּא הָיָה אוֹמֵר: הַיִּלּוֹדִים לָמוּת, וְהַמֵּתִים לְהַחֲיוֹת, וְהַחַיִּים לִדּוֹן, לֵדַע וּלְהוֹדִיעַ וּלְהִוָּדַע שֶׁהוּא אֵל. הוּא הַיּוֹצֵר, הוּא הַבּוֹרֵא, הוּא הַמֵּבִין, הוּא הַדַּיָּן, הוּא הָעֵד, הוּא בַּעַל דִּין, הוּא עָתִיד לָדוּן. בָּרוּךְ הוּא, שֶׁאֵין לְפָנָיו לֹא עַוְלָה, וְלֹא שִׁכְחָה, וְלֹא מַשּׂוֹא פָנִים, וְלֹא מִקַּח שֹׁחַד. וְדַע שֶׁהַכֹּל לְפִי הַחֶשְׁבּוֹן. וְאַל יַבְטִיחֲךָ יִצְרְךָ שֶׁהַשְּׁאוֹל בֵּית מָנוֹס לָךְ, שֶׁעַל כָּרְחֲךָ אַתָּה נוֹצָר, וְעַל כָּרְחֲךָ אַתָּה נוֹלָד, וְעַל כָּרְחֲךָ אַתָּה חַי, וְעַל כָּרְחֲךָ אַתָּה מֵת, וְעַל כָּרְחֲךָ אַתָּה עָתִיד לִתֵּן דִּין וְחֶשְׁבּוֹן לִפְנֵי מֶלֶךְ מַלְכֵי הַמְּלָכִים, הַקָּדוֹשׁ בָּרוּךְ הוּא.

רַבִּי חֲנַנְיָא בֶּן עֲקַשְׁיָא אוֹמֵר: רָצָה הַקָּדוֹשׁ בָּרוּךְ הוּא לְזַכּוֹת אֶת יִשְׂרָאֵל, לְפִיכָךְ הִרְבָּה לָהֶם תּוֹרָה וּמִצְוֹת, שֶׁנֶּאֱמַר: יְיָ חָפֵץ לְמַעַן צִדְקוֹ, יַגְדִּיל תּוֹרָה וְיַאְדִּיר.

פֶּרֶק חֲמִישִׁי

כָּל יִשְׂרָאֵל יֵשׁ לָהֶם חֵלֶק לְעוֹלָם הַבָּא, שֶׁנֶּאֱמַר: וְעַמֵּךְ כֻּלָּם צַדִּיקִים, לְעוֹלָם יִירְשׁוּ אָרֶץ; נֵצֶר מַטָּעַי, מַעֲשֵׂה יָדַי לְהִתְפָּאֵר.

א. בַּעֲשָׂרָה מַאֲמָרוֹת נִבְרָא הָעוֹלָם. וּמַה תַּלְמוּד לוֹמַר, וַהֲלֹא בְּמַאֲמָר אֶחָד יָכוֹל לְהִבָּרְאוֹת, אֶלָּא לְהִפָּרַע מִן הָרְשָׁעִים, שֶׁמְּאַבְּדִים אֶת הָעוֹלָם שֶׁנִּבְרָא בַּעֲשָׂרָה מַאֲמָרוֹת, וְלִתֵּן שָׂכָר טוֹב לַצַּדִּיקִים, שֶׁמְּקַיְּמִים אֶת הָעוֹלָם שֶׁנִּבְרָא בַּעֲשָׂרָה מַאֲמָרוֹת.

רבי אלעזר הקפר, father of Bar Kappara, lived in the second century. מקח שחד. The Mishnah text has שהכל שלו after the words לחיות=להחיות.

28. Rabbi Elazar ha-Kappar said: Envy, lust and vainglory shorten a man's life.

29. He used to say: Those who are born are destined to die; those who are dead are destined to be brought to life again; and the living are destined to be judged. [It is for you] to know, proclaim and be sure that he is God. He is the Maker, he the Creator, he the Discerner, he the Judge, he the Witness, he the Complainant; it is he who will judge. Blessed be he in whose presence there is no wrongdoing, nor forgetting, nor partiality, nor taking of bribes. Know that all is according to reckoning, and let not your imagination persuade you that the grave is a place of refuge for you. Perforce you were formed and perforce you were born; perforce you live, perforce you shall die, and perforce you shall have to give a strict account before the supreme King of kings, the Holy One, blessed be he.

Rabbi Ḥananyah ben Akashyah said: The Holy One, blessed be he, desired to purify Israel; hence he gave them a Torah rich in rules of conduct, as it is said: "The Lord was pleased, for the sake of [Israel's] righteousness, to render the Torah great and glorious."[1]

CHAPTER FIVE

All Israel have a share in the world to come, as it is said: "Your people shall all be righteous; they shall possess the land forever; they are a plant of my own, the work of my hands, wherein I may glory."[2]

1. By ten divine utterances was the world created. Why does the Torah indicate this? Surely the world could have been created by one divine utterance. It means to emphasize that God will exact [severe] penalty from the wicked who destroy the world which was created by [no less than] ten utterances, and that he will grant a rich reward to the righteous who maintain the world which was created by ten utterances.

בעשרה מאמרות The several phases of creation are introduced by the phrase "and God said" nine times in Genesis 1:3–29 and once in 2:18.

The paragraphs in this chapter, arranged under several numerical headings, are of unknown authorship and folkloristic in nature.

---

[1] *Isaiah* 42:21.   [2] *Isaiah* 60:21.

ב. עֲשָׂרָה דוֹרוֹת מֵאָדָם וְעַד נֹחַ, לְהוֹדִיעַ כַּמָּה אֹרֶךְ
אַפַּיִם לְפָנָיו, שֶׁכָּל הַדּוֹרוֹת הָיוּ מַכְעִיסִים לְפָנָיו, עַד שֶׁהֵבִיא
עֲלֵיהֶם אֶת מֵי הַמַּבּוּל.

ג. עֲשָׂרָה דוֹרוֹת מִנֹּחַ וְעַד אַבְרָהָם, לְהוֹדִיעַ כַּמָּה אֹרֶךְ
אַפַּיִם לְפָנָיו, שֶׁכָּל הַדּוֹרוֹת הָיוּ מַכְעִיסִים לְפָנָיו, עַד שֶׁבָּא
אַבְרָהָם אָבִינוּ וְקִבֵּל שְׂכַר כֻּלָּם.

ד. עֲשָׂרָה נִסְיוֹנוֹת נִתְנַסָּה אַבְרָהָם אָבִינוּ וְעָמַד בְּכֻלָּם,
לְהוֹדִיעַ כַּמָּה חִבָּתוֹ שֶׁל אַבְרָהָם אָבִינוּ.

ה. עֲשָׂרָה נִסִּים נַעֲשׂוּ לַאֲבוֹתֵינוּ בְמִצְרַיִם, וַעֲשָׂרָה עַל
הַיָּם. אֲשֶׁר מַכּוֹת הֵבִיא הַקָּדוֹשׁ בָּרוּךְ הוּא עַל הַמִּצְרִים
בְּמִצְרַיִם, וְעֶשֶׂר עַל הַיָּם.

ו. עֲשָׂרָה נִסְיוֹנוֹת נִסּוּ אֲבוֹתֵינוּ אֶת הַקָּדוֹשׁ בָּרוּךְ הוּא
בַמִּדְבָּר, שֶׁנֶּאֱמַר: וַיְנַסּוּ אֹתִי זֶה עֶשֶׂר פְּעָמִים, וְלֹא שָׁמְעוּ
בְּקוֹלִי.

ז. עֲשָׂרָה נִסִּים נַעֲשׂוּ לַאֲבוֹתֵינוּ בְּבֵית הַמִּקְדָּשׁ: לֹא הִפִּילָה
אִשָּׁה מֵרֵיחַ בְּשַׂר הַקֹּדֶשׁ, וְלֹא הִסְרִיחַ בְּשַׂר הַקֹּדֶשׁ מֵעוֹלָם,
וְלֹא נִרְאָה זְבוּב בְּבֵית הַמִּטְבְּחַיִם, וְלֹא אֵרַע קֶרִי לְכֹהֵן גָּדוֹל
בְּיוֹם הַכִּפּוּרִים, וְלֹא כִבּוּ הַגְּשָׁמִים אֵשׁ שֶׁל עֲצֵי הַמַּעֲרָכָה,
וְלֹא נִצְּחָה הָרוּחַ אֶת עַמּוּד הֶעָשָׁן, וְלֹא נִמְצָא פְּסוּל בָּעֹמֶר
וּבִשְׁתֵּי הַלֶּחֶם וּבְלֶחֶם הַפָּנִים, עוֹמְדִים צְפוּפִים וּמִשְׁתַּחֲוִים
רְוָחִים, וְלֹא הִזִּיק נָחָשׁ וְעַקְרָב בִּירוּשָׁלַיִם מֵעוֹלָם, וְלֹא אָמַר
אָדָם לַחֲבֵרוֹ צַר לִי הַמָּקוֹם שֶׁאָלִין בִּירוּשָׁלָיִם.

לחם הפנים ("bread of presence"), the unleavened bread which the priests
placed before the Lord in the sanctuary (Exodus 25:30). This consisted of
twelve loaves, representing the twelve tribes of Israel, and was expressive of
man's constant indebtedness to God who is the source of every material
blessing. It had to be baked before the Sabbath; if there had been anything

2. The ten generations from Adam to Noah [are recorded in Genesis] to make known how great is God's patience; for all those generations continued provoking him, until he [finally] brought upon them the waters of the flood.

3. The ten generations from Noah to Abraham [are recorded] to make known how great is God's patience; for all those generations continued provoking him, until our father Abraham came and received the reward they should all have been given [had they not forfeited their share].

4. With ten trials was our father Abraham tried, and he stood firm in all of them; [this is recorded] to make known how great was the love of our father Abraham [towards God].

5. Ten miracles were performed for our fathers in Egypt, and ten at the Red Sea [the plagues did no harm to the Israelites]. Ten plagues did the Holy One, blessed be he, bring upon the Egyptians in Egypt, and ten at the Sea.

6. With ten trials did our fathers try the Holy One, blessed be he, in the wilderness, as it is said: "They have put me to the test ten times now, and have not obeyed my voice."

7. Ten miracles were done for our fathers in the Sanctuary: no woman miscarried from the scent of the sacrificial meat; the sacrificial meat never became putrid; no fly was seen in the slaughter-house; no unclean accident ever happened to the high priest on the Day of Atonement; the rain never extinguished the fire of the wood-pile [on the altar, which was under the open sky]; the wind did not prevail against the column of smoke [from the altar-fire, so that the smoke was not blown downward]; no disqualifying defect was ever found in the *Omer* [of new barley, offered on the second day of Passover], or in the two loaves [baked of the First Fruits of the wheat-harvest and offered up on Pentecost], or in the shewbread [which was changed weekly, on the Sabbath]; though the people stood closely pressed together, they found ample space to prostrate themselves; never did a serpent or scorpion do injury in Jerusalem; and no man ever said to his fellow: "I have not room to lodge overnight in Jerusalem."

---

wrong with it, they could not have changed the bread for another week. Similarly, if the עומר had been found defective, it would have been impossible to provide another supply in time for the offering. The baking of the two loaves of בכורים had to be done before the commencement of the *Shavuoth* festival; if they had been defective, others could not have been offered on the altar.

ח. עֲשָׂרָה דְבָרִים נִבְרְאוּ בְּעֶרֶב שַׁבָּת בֵּין הַשְּׁמָשׁוֹת, וְאֵלוּ
הֵן: פִּי הָאָרֶץ, פִּי הַבְּאֵר, פִּי הָאָתוֹן, הַקֶּשֶׁת, וְהַמָּן, וְהַמַּטֶּה,
וְהַשָּׁמִיר, הַכְּתָב, וְהַמִּכְתָּב, וְהַלֻּחוֹת. וְיֵשׁ אוֹמְרִים: אַף
הַמַּזִּיקִין, וּקְבוּרָתוֹ שֶׁל מֹשֶׁה, וְאֵילוֹ שֶׁל אַבְרָהָם אָבִינוּ. וְיֵשׁ
אוֹמְרִים: אַף צְבָת בִּצְבָת עֲשׂוּיָה.

ט. שִׁבְעָה דְבָרִים בְּגֹלֶם, וְשִׁבְעָה בְּחָכָם: חָכָם אֵינוֹ מְדַבֵּר
לִפְנֵי מִי שֶׁגָּדוֹל מִמֶּנּוּ בְּחָכְמָה (וּבְמִנְיָן), וְאֵינוֹ נִכְנָס לְתוֹךְ דִּבְרֵי
חֲבֵרוֹ, וְאֵינוֹ נִבְהָל לְהָשִׁיב, שׁוֹאֵל כְּעִנְיָן וּמֵשִׁיב כַּהֲלָכָה,
וְאוֹמֵר עַל רִאשׁוֹן רִאשׁוֹן וְעַל אַחֲרוֹן אַחֲרוֹן, וְעַל מַה שֶּׁלֹּא
שָׁמַע אוֹמֵר לֹא שָׁמַעְתִּי, וּמוֹדֶה עַל הָאֱמֶת; וְחִלּוּפֵיהֶם בְּגֹלֶם.

י. שִׁבְעָה מִינֵי פֻּרְעָנִיּוֹת בָּאִים לָעוֹלָם עַל שִׁבְעָה גוּפֵי
עֲבֵרָה: מִקְצָתָם מְעַשְּׂרִים וּמִקְצָתָם אֵינָם מְעַשְּׂרִים, רָעָב שֶׁל
בַּצֹּרֶת בָּא, מִקְצָתָם רְעֵבִים וּמִקְצָתָם שְׂבֵעִים. גָּמְרוּ שֶׁלֹּא
לְעַשֵּׂר, רָעָב שֶׁל מְהוּמָה וְשֶׁל בַּצֹּרֶת בָּא; וְשֶׁלֹּא לִטּוֹל אֶת
הַחַלָּה, רָעָב שֶׁל כְּלָיָה בָּא.

יא. דֶּבֶר בָּא לָעוֹלָם עַל מִיתוֹת הָאֲמוּרוֹת בַּתּוֹרָה שֶׁלֹּא
נִמְסְרוּ לְבֵית דִּין, וְעַל פֵּרוֹת שְׁבִיעִית. חֶרֶב בָּאָה לָעוֹלָם
עַל עִנּוּי הַדִּין, וְעַל עִוּוּת הַדִּין, וְעַל הַמּוֹרִים בַּתּוֹרָה שֶׁלֹּא
כַהֲלָכָה. חַיָּה רָעָה בָּאָה לָעוֹלָם עַל שְׁבוּעַת שָׁוְא וְעַל חִלּוּל
הַשֵּׁם. גָּלוּת בָּאָה לָעוֹלָם עַל עֲבוֹדַת כּוֹכָבִים, וְעַל גִּלּוּי
עֲרָיוֹת, וְעַל שְׁפִיכוּת דָּמִים, וְעַל שְׁמִטַּת הָאָרֶץ.

בין השמשות at the end of the six days of creation, prior to the first Sabbath.

שמיר in Jeremiah 17:1 means a hard flint used for engraving. In rab-
binic literature it denotes a tiny worm able to split the hardest stone. King
Solomon is said to have employed the *Shamir* in view of the command that
no iron tool be used at the building of an altar to God (Exodus 20:22), "for
iron was created to shorten man's life, whereas the altar was created to pro-
long man's life" (Middoth 3:4).

8.   Ten things were created on the eve of Sabbath at twilight,
namely: the mouth of the earth [which engulfed Korah]; the mouth
of the well [which supplied the Israelites with water in the wilder-
ness]; the mouth of the ass [which spoke to Balaam]; the rainbow
[given as a sign after the flood]; the manna [dropped from heaven];
the rod [of Moses]; the *shamir* [employed for splitting stones at
the building of the Temple]; the shape of the written characters;
the engraving instrument; and the tablets of stone. Some include
also the demons, the grave of Moses, and the ram of our father
Abraham; others include also the original tongs, for tongs can [in
human experience] be made only by means of tongs.

9.   There are seven characteristics of a stupid person, and
seven of a wise man. The wise man does not speak in the presence of
one who is greater than he in wisdom; he does not interrupt the
speech of his companion; he is not hasty to answer; he questions
and answers properly, to the point; he speaks on the first point
first, and on the last point last; regarding that which he has not
learnt he says: "I have not learnt"; and he acknowledges the truth.
The opposites of these traits are to be found in a stupid person.

10.   Seven kinds of punishment come to the world for seven
capital transgressions. When some people give tithes and others
do not, there comes a famine from lack of rain; then some go
hungry and others have plenty. If all have decided not to give
tithes, there comes a famine from panic of war and drought; if
they have further resolved not to set apart the dough-cake [for
the priest], there comes a famine of extermination.

11.   Pestilence comes to the world to inflict those death pen-
alties mentioned in the Torah, the execution of which is not within
the function of a human tribunal, and for making forbidden use
of the harvest of the Sabbatical year. The sword comes to the
world for the suppression [or delay] of justice, and for the perversion
of justice, and on account of those who misinterpret the Torah.
Wild beasts come to the world on account of perjury, and for the
profanation of God's name. Exile comes to the world on account
of idolatry, incest, bloodshed, and for not allowing the soil to rest
in the Sabbatical year.

. . . הכתב the writing on the tablets, the instrument with which it was
written, and the tablets themselves.

צבת בצבת עשויה that is, all unexplained beginnings as well as everything
supernatural resulted from the original Cause—God.

יב. בְּאַרְבָּעָה פְרָקִים הַדֶּבֶר מִתְרַבֶּה: בָּרְבִיעִית,
וּבַשְּׁבִיעִית, וּבְמוֹצָאֵי שְׁבִיעִית, וּבְמוֹצָאֵי הֶחָג שֶׁבְּכָל שָׁנָה וְשָׁנָה.
בָּרְבִיעִית, מִפְּנֵי מַעְשַׂר עָנִי שֶׁבַּשְּׁלִישִׁית; בַּשְּׁבִיעִית, מִפְּנֵי
מַעְשַׂר עָנִי שֶׁבַּשִּׁשִּׁית; בְּמוֹצָאֵי שְׁבִיעִית, מִפְּנֵי פֵּרוֹת שְׁבִיעִית;
בְּמוֹצָאֵי הֶחָג שֶׁבְּכָל שָׁנָה וְשָׁנָה, מִפְּנֵי גֶּזֶל מַתְּנוֹת עֲנִיִּים.

יג. אַרְבַּע מִדּוֹת בָּאָדָם: הָאוֹמֵר שֶׁלִּי שֶׁלִּי וְשֶׁלְּךָ שֶׁלָּךְ, זוֹ
מִדָּה בֵינוֹנִית, וְיֵשׁ אוֹמְרִים זוֹ מִדַּת סְדוֹם; שֶׁלִּי שֶׁלָּךְ וְשֶׁלְּךָ
שֶׁלִּי, עַם הָאָרֶץ; שֶׁלִּי שֶׁלָּךְ וְשֶׁלְּךָ שֶׁלָּךְ, חָסִיד; שֶׁלְּךָ שֶׁלִּי
וְשֶׁלִּי שֶׁלִּי, רָשָׁע.

יד. אַרְבַּע מִדּוֹת בַּדֵּעוֹת: נוֹחַ לִכְעֹס וְנוֹחַ לִרְצוֹת, יָצָא
הֶפְסֵדוֹ בִשְׂכָרוֹ; קָשֶׁה לִכְעֹס וְקָשֶׁה לִרְצוֹת, יָצָא שְׂכָרוֹ
בְהֶפְסֵדוֹ; קָשֶׁה לִכְעֹס וְנוֹחַ לִרְצוֹת, חָסִיד; נוֹחַ לִכְעֹס וְקָשֶׁה
לִרְצוֹת, רָשָׁע.

טו. אַרְבַּע מִדּוֹת בַּתַּלְמִידִים: מָהִיר לִשְׁמֹעַ וּמָהִיר לְאַבֵּד,
יָצָא שְׂכָרוֹ בְהֶפְסֵדוֹ; קָשֶׁה לִשְׁמֹעַ וְקָשֶׁה לְאַבֵּד, יָצָא הֶפְסֵדוֹ
בִשְׂכָרוֹ; מָהִיר לִשְׁמֹעַ וְקָשֶׁה לְאַבֵּד, זֶה חֵלֶק טוֹב; קָשֶׁה לִשְׁמֹעַ
וּמָהִיר לְאַבֵּד, זֶה חֵלֶק רָע.

מעשר עני, a tenth part of the third and sixth years' income, was given to "the Levite, the stranger, the fatherless, and the widow" (Deuteronomy 14:28–29).

גזל מתנות עניים The right of proprietorship does not extend to the corners of the field, the gleanings of the harvest, and the forgotten sheaf; these belong to the poor people (Leviticus 19:9–10; 23:22).

מדות qualitative measures, standards by which a person may be judged.

האומר שלי שלי The man who neither gives nor takes is neither good nor bad, but intermediate. Since, however, he is indifferent to the welfare of others, there are some who regard him as a type of Sodom notorious for corruption and selfishness.

12.   At four periods pestilence increases: in the fourth year, in the seventh [Sabbatical] year, in the year following the Sabbatical year, and at the conclusion of the Feast of Tabernacles in every year. In the fourth year, for having failed to give the tithe to the poor which was due in the third year; in the seventh year, for having failed to give the tithe to the poor which was due in the sixth year; in the year following the Sabbatical year, for having made forbidden use of the harvest of the Sabbatical year; at the conclusion of the Feast of Tabernacles in every year, for having robbed the gifts assigned to the poor [in the course of the whole agricultural year].

13.   There are four characters among men: He who says: "What is mine is mine, and what is yours is yours" is the average type, though some say this is a Sodom-type; he who says: "What is mine is yours, and what is yours is mine" is ignorant; he who says: "What is mine is yours, and what is yours is yours" is godly; he who says: "What is yours is mine, and what is mine is mine" is wicked.

14.   There are four kinds of dispositions: Easy to become angry and easy to be pacified, his loss is compensated by his gain; hard to become angry and hard to be pacified, his gain is offset by his loss; hard to become angry and easy to be pacified is godly; easy to become angry and hard to be pacified is wicked.

15.   There are four types of students: Quick to learn and quick to forget, his gain is offset by his loss; slow to learn and slow to forget, his loss is compensated by his gain; quick to learn and slow to forget is the best quality; slow to learn and quick to forget is the worst quality.

עם הארץ who does not know that one must do good to others unconditionally, without a view to recompense.

ארבע מדות בתלמידים The types of students described in paragraph 18 are: the sponge, absorbing indiscriminately everything, the true and the false; the funnel, retaining none of the subjects learned; the strainer, retaining what is useless and forgetting what is useful; the sieve, retaining what is best.

טז. אַרְבַּע מִדּוֹת בְּנוֹתְנֵי צְדָקָה: הָרוֹצֶה שֶׁיִּתֵּן וְלֹא יִתְּנוּ אֲחֵרִים, עֵינוֹ רָעָה בְּשֶׁל אֲחֵרִים; יִתְּנוּ אֲחֵרִים וְהוּא לֹא יִתֵּן, עֵינוֹ רָעָה בְּשֶׁלּוֹ; יִתֵּן וְיִתְּנוּ אֲחֵרִים, חָסִיד; לֹא יִתֵּן וְלֹא יִתְּנוּ אֲחֵרִים, רָשָׁע.

יז. אַרְבַּע מִדּוֹת בְּהוֹלְכֵי בֵית הַמִּדְרָשׁ: הוֹלֵךְ וְאֵינוֹ עוֹשֶׂה, שְׂכַר הֲלִיכָה בְּיָדוֹ; עוֹשֶׂה וְאֵינוֹ הוֹלֵךְ, שְׂכַר מַעֲשֶׂה בְּיָדוֹ; הוֹלֵךְ וְעוֹשֶׂה, חָסִיד; לֹא הוֹלֵךְ וְלֹא עוֹשֶׂה, רָשָׁע.

יח. אַרְבַּע מִדּוֹת בְּיוֹשְׁבִים לִפְנֵי חֲכָמִים: סְפוֹג, וּמַשְׁפֵּךְ, מְשַׁמֶּרֶת, וְנָפָה. סְפוֹג, שֶׁהוּא סוֹפֵג אֶת הַכֹּל; וּמַשְׁפֵּךְ, שֶׁמַּכְנִיס בְּזוֹ וּמוֹצִיא בְזוֹ; מְשַׁמֶּרֶת, שֶׁמּוֹצִיאָה אֶת הַיַּיִן וְקוֹלֶטֶת אֶת הַשְּׁמָרִים; וְנָפָה, שֶׁמּוֹצִיאָה אֶת הַקֶּמַח וְקוֹלֶטֶת אֶת הַסֹּלֶת.

יט. כָּל אַהֲבָה שֶׁהִיא תְלוּיָה בְדָבָר, בָּטֵל דָּבָר בְּטֵלָה אַהֲבָה; וְשֶׁאֵינָה תְּלוּיָה בְדָבָר, אֵינָהּ בְּטֵלָה לְעוֹלָם. אֵיזוֹ הִיא אַהֲבָה שֶׁהִיא תְלוּיָה בְדָבָר, זוֹ אַהֲבַת אַמְנוֹן וְתָמָר; וְשֶׁאֵינָהּ תְּלוּיָה בְדָבָר, זוֹ אַהֲבַת דָּוִד וִיהוֹנָתָן.

כ. כָּל מַחֲלֹקֶת שֶׁהִיא לְשֵׁם שָׁמַיִם, סוֹפָהּ לְהִתְקַיֵּם; וְשֶׁאֵינָהּ לְשֵׁם שָׁמַיִם, אֵין סוֹפָהּ לְהִתְקַיֵּם. אֵיזוֹ הִיא מַחֲלֹקֶת שֶׁהִיא לְשֵׁם שָׁמַיִם, זוֹ מַחֲלֹקֶת הִלֵּל וְשַׁמַּי; וְשֶׁאֵינָהּ לְשֵׁם שָׁמַיִם, זוֹ מַחֲלֹקֶת קֹרַח וְכָל עֲדָתוֹ.

כא. כָּל הַמְזַכֶּה אֶת הָרַבִּים, אֵין חֵטְא בָּא עַל יָדוֹ; וְכָל הַמַּחֲטִיא אֶת הָרַבִּים, אֵין מַסְפִּיקִים בְּיָדוֹ לַעֲשׂוֹת תְּשׁוּבָה. מֹשֶׁה זָכָה וְזִכָּה אֶת הָרַבִּים, זְכוּת הָרַבִּים תְּלוּיָה בּוֹ, שֶׁנֶּאֱמַר: צִדְקַת יְיָ עָשָׂה, וּמִשְׁפָּטָיו עִם יִשְׂרָאֵל. יָרָבְעָם בֶּן נְבָט חָטָא וְהֶחֱטִיא אֶת הָרַבִּים, חֵטְא הָרַבִּים תָּלוּי בּוֹ, שֶׁנֶּאֱמַר: עַל חַטֹּאות יָרָבְעָם אֲשֶׁר חָטָא וַאֲשֶׁר הֶחֱטִיא אֶת יִשְׂרָאֵל.

קמח here denotes superfine dust of useless quality (Maimonides).

16.   There are four types of donors to charity: He who gives
and does not want others to give begrudges others; he who wants
others to give but will not give himself begrudges himself; he who
gives and wants others to give is saintly; he who will not give and
does not want others to give is wicked.

17.   There are four types of those who attend school: He who
attends and does not practise [the teachings of the school] secures
the reward for attending; he who practises [leading a good life] but
does not attend [to acquire knowledge] secures the reward for
practising; he who attends and practises is saintly; he who neither
attends nor practises is wicked.

18.   There are four types of those who sit in the presence of
sages: the sponge, the funnel, the strainer, and the sieve. The sponge
absorbs all; the funnel receives at one end and spills out at the
other; the strainer lets the wine through and retains the dregs; and
the sieve lets out the flour dust and retains the fine flour.

19.   All love which depends on sensual attraction will pass
away as soon as the sensual attraction disappears; but if it is not
dependent on sensual attraction, it will never pass away. Which
love was dependent on sensual attraction? The love of Amnon and
Tamar. And which depended on nothing selfish? The love of
David and Jonathan.

20.   Any controversy which is in the name of Heaven [from
sincere motive] is destined to result in something permanent; any
controversy which is not in the name of Heaven will never result
in anything permanent. Which controversy was in the name of
Heaven? The controversy between Hillel and Shammai. And which
was not in the name of Heaven? The controversy of Korah and
all his company.

21.   Whoever leads the people to righteousness, no sin shall
occur through him; whoever leads the people to sin shall not be
enabled to repent. Moses was righteous and led the people to
righteousness, hence the merit of the people is attributed to him,
as it is said: "He performed the justice of the Lord, and his ordi-
nances with Israel."[1] Jeroboam, the son of Nebat, sinned and
caused others to sin, hence the sin of the people is attributed to
him, as it is said: "For the sins of Jeroboam which he sinned and
caused Israel to sin."[2]

---

[1] *Deuteronomy* 33:21.   [2] *I Kings* 15:30.

כב. כָּל מִי שֶׁיֶּשׁ־בּוֹ שְׁלֹשָׁה דְבָרִים הַלָּלוּ הוּא מִתַּלְמִידָיו שֶׁל אַבְרָהָם אָבִינוּ, וּשְׁלֹשָׁה דְבָרִים אֲחֵרִים, הוּא מִתַּלְמִידָיו שֶׁל בִּלְעָם הָרָשָׁע. עַיִן טוֹבָה, וְרוּחַ נְמוּכָה, וְנֶפֶשׁ שְׁפָלָה, מִתַּלְמִידָיו שֶׁל אַבְרָהָם אָבִינוּ; עַיִן רָעָה, וְרוּחַ גְּבוֹהָה, וְנֶפֶשׁ רְחָבָה, מִתַּלְמִידָיו שֶׁל בִּלְעָם הָרָשָׁע. מַה בֵּין תַּלְמִידָיו שֶׁל אַבְרָהָם אָבִינוּ לְתַלְמִידָיו שֶׁל בִּלְעָם הָרָשָׁע, תַּלְמִידָיו שֶׁל אַבְרָהָם אָבִינוּ אוֹכְלִים בָּעוֹלָם הַזֶּה וְנוֹחֲלִים הָעוֹלָם הַבָּא, שֶׁנֶּאֱמַר: לְהַנְחִיל אֹהֲבַי יֵשׁ, וְאֹצְרֹתֵיהֶם אֲמַלֵּא. אֲבָל תַּלְמִידָיו שֶׁל בִּלְעָם הָרָשָׁע יוֹרְשִׁים גֵּיהִנֹּם וְיוֹרְדִים לִבְאֵר שָׁחַת, שֶׁנֶּאֱמַר: וְאַתָּה, אֱלֹהִים, תּוֹרִדֵם לִבְאֵר שַׁחַת, אַנְשֵׁי דָמִים וּמִרְמָה, לֹא יֶחֱצוּ יְמֵיהֶם, וַאֲנִי אֶבְטַח בָּךְ.

כג. יְהוּדָה בֶן תֵּימָא אוֹמֵר: הֱוֵי עַז כַּנָּמֵר, וְקַל כַּנֶּשֶׁר, רָץ כַּצְּבִי, וְגִבּוֹר כָּאֲרִי, לַעֲשׂוֹת רְצוֹן אָבִיךְ שֶׁבַּשָּׁמָיִם. הוּא הָיָה אוֹמֵר: עַז פָּנִים לְגֵיהִנֹּם, וּבוֹשׁ פָּנִים לְגַן עֵדֶן.

יְהִי רָצוֹן מִלְּפָנֶיךָ, יְיָ אֱלֹהֵינוּ וֵאלֹהֵי אֲבוֹתֵינוּ, שֶׁיִּבָּנֶה בֵּית הַמִּקְדָּשׁ בִּמְהֵרָה בְיָמֵינוּ, וְתֵן חֶלְקֵנוּ בְּתוֹרָתֶךָ.

כד. הוּא הָיָה אוֹמֵר: בֶּן חָמֵשׁ שָׁנִים לַמִּקְרָא, בֶּן עֶשֶׂר שָׁנִים לַמִּשְׁנָה, בֶּן שְׁלֹשׁ עֶשְׂרֵה לַמִּצְוֹת, בֶּן חֲמֵשׁ עֶשְׂרֵה לַתַּלְמוּד, בֶּן שְׁמֹנֶה עֶשְׂרֵה לַחֻפָּה, בֶּן עֶשְׂרִים לִרְדֹּף, בֶּן שְׁלֹשִׁים לַכֹּחַ, בֶּן אַרְבָּעִים לַבִּינָה, בֶּן חֲמִשִּׁים לְעֵצָה, בֶּן שִׁשִּׁים לְזִקְנָה, בֶּן שִׁבְעִים לְשֵׂיבָה, בֶּן שְׁמוֹנִים לִגְבוּרָה, בֶּן תִּשְׁעִים לָשׁוּחַ, בֶּן מֵאָה כְּאִלּוּ מֵת וְעָבַר וּבָטֵל מִן הָעוֹלָם.

יֵשׁ ("substance") numerically equals 310. This word is here homiletically represented as referring to the 310 worlds which are believed to be meant for the righteous in the hereafter.

22. Whoever possesses the following three qualities is of the disciples of our father Abraham; whoever possesses the opposite three qualities is of the disciples of the wicked Balaam. Those who belong to the disciples of our father Abraham possess a good eye [generous nature], a humble spirit, and a modest desire. Those who belong to the disciples of the wicked Balaam possess an evil eye [grudging nature], a haughty spirit, and an excessive desire [for wealth]. What is the difference between the disciples of our father Abraham and the disciples of the wicked Balaam? The disciples of our father Abraham enjoy this world and inherit the world to come, as it is said: "Endowing my friends with wealth, I fill their treasures."[1] But the disciples of the wicked Balaam inherit *Gehinnom* and descend into the nethermost pit, as it is said: "Thou, O God, wilt bring them down into the nethermost pit; men of blood and fraud shall not live out half their days; as for me, I trust in thee."[2]

23.   Judah ben Tema said: Be bold as a leopard, light as an eagle, swift as a deer, and strong as a lion, to do the will of your Father who is in heaven. He used to say: The impudent is destined for *Gehinnom*, but the shamefaced is destined for paradise.

May it be thy will, Lord our God and God of our fathers, that the Temple be rebuilt speedily in our days, and grant us a share in thy Torah.

24.   He used to say: At five years the age is reached for the study of Bible, at ten for the study of Mishnah, at thirteen for the fulfillment of the commandments, at fifteen for the study of Talmud, at eighteen for marriage, at twenty for seeking a livelihood, at thirty for full strength, at forty for understanding, at fifty for giving counsel; at sixty a man attains old age, at seventy white old age, at eighty rare old age; at ninety he is bending over the grave; at a hundred he is as if he were already dead and had passed away from the world.

יהודה בן תימא probably lived towards the end of the second century, and belonged to the fifth and last generation of the *Tannaim*. His name occurs only once in the Mishnah.

יהי רצון should be at the end of the chapter, according to the Wilna Gaon.

לשׁוּח is rendered here in the combined sense of שׁוּחה ("grave") and שׁחה ("to bend").

[1] *Proverbs* 8:21.   [2] *Psalm* 55:24.

כה. בֶּן בַּג בַּג אוֹמֵר: הֲפָךְ־בַּהּ וַהֲפָךְ־בַּהּ דְּכֹלָּא בַהּ, וּבַהּ תֶּחֱזֵא, וְסִיב וּבְלֵה בַהּ, וּמִנַּהּ לָא תָזוּעַ, שֶׁאֵין לְךָ מִדָּה טוֹבָה הֵימֶנָּה.

כו. בֶּן הֵא הֵא אוֹמֵר: לְפֻם צַעֲרָא אַגְרָא.

רַבִּי חֲנַנְיָא בֶּן עֲקַשְׁיָא אוֹמֵר: רָצָה הַקָּדוֹשׁ בָּרוּךְ הוּא לְזַכּוֹת אֶת יִשְׂרָאֵל, לְפִיכָךְ הִרְבָּה לָהֶם תּוֹרָה וּמִצְוֹת, שֶׁנֶּאֱמַר: יְיָ חָפֵץ לְמַעַן צִדְקוֹ, יַגְדִּיל תּוֹרָה וְיַאְדִּיר.

פֶּרֶק שִׁשִּׁי

כָּל יִשְׂרָאֵל יֵשׁ לָהֶם חֵלֶק לָעוֹלָם הַבָּא, שֶׁנֶּאֱמַר: וְעַמֵּךְ כֻּלָּם צַדִּיקִים, לְעוֹלָם יִירְשׁוּ אָרֶץ; נֵצֶר מַטָּעַי, מַעֲשֵׂה יָדַי לְהִתְפָּאֵר.

שָׁנוּ חֲכָמִים בִּלְשׁוֹן הַמִּשְׁנָה; בָּרוּךְ שֶׁבָּחַר בָּהֶם וּבְמִשְׁנָתָם.

א. רַבִּי מֵאִיר אוֹמֵר: כָּל הָעוֹסֵק בַּתּוֹרָה לִשְׁמָהּ זוֹכֶה לִדְבָרִים הַרְבֵּה; וְלֹא עוֹד, אֶלָּא שֶׁכָּל הָעוֹלָם כֻּלּוֹ כְּדַי הוּא לוֹ: נִקְרָא רֵעַ, אָהוּב, אוֹהֵב אֶת הַמָּקוֹם, אוֹהֵב אֶת הַבְּרִיּוֹת, מְשַׂמֵּחַ אֶת הַמָּקוֹם, מְשַׂמֵּחַ אֶת הַבְּרִיּוֹת. וּמַלְבַּשְׁתּוֹ עֲנָוָה וְיִרְאָה, וּמַכְשַׁרְתּוֹ לִהְיוֹת צַדִּיק, חָסִיד, יָשָׁר וְנֶאֱמָן; וּמְרַחַקְתּוֹ מִן הַחֵטְא, וּמְקָרַבְתּוֹ לִידֵי זְכוּת. וְנֶהֱנִין מִמֶּנּוּ עֵצָה וְתוּשִׁיָּה, בִּינָה וּגְבוּרָה, שֶׁנֶּאֱמַר: לִי עֵצָה וְתוּשִׁיָּה, אֲנִי בִינָה, לִי גְבוּרָה. וְנוֹתֶנֶת לוֹ מַלְכוּת וּמֶמְשָׁלָה, וְחִקּוּר דִּין. וּמְגַלִּים לוֹ רָזֵי

<hr>

בֶּן הֵא הֵא and בֶּן בַּג בַּג are said to have been disciples of Hillel, and prose-lytes. There is a fanciful explanation to the effect that Ben Hé-Hé denotes a spiritual son of Abraham and Sarah, whose names God altered by the in-sertion of the letter ה (Abram's name was changed to Abraham, and that of Sarai to Sarah). Since the numerical value of בג is equivalent to ה (five), it is said that בֶּן בַּג בַּג is equivalent to בֶּן הֵא הֵא, and that both are epithets of prose-lytes (Tosafoth, Ḥagigah 9b).

25.   Ben Bag-Bag said: Study the Torah again and again, for everything is contained in it; constantly examine it, grow old and gray over it, and swerve not from it, for there is nothing more excellent than it.

26.   Ben Hé-Hé said: According to the effort is the reward.

Rabbi Ḥananyah ben Akashyah said: The Holy One, blessed be he, desired to purify Israel; hence he gave them a Torah rich in rules of conduct, as it is said: "The Lord was pleased, for the sake of [Israel's] righteousness, to render the Torah great and glorious."[1]

CHAPTER SIX

All Israel have a share in the world to come, as it is said: "Your people shall all be righteous; they shall possess the land forever; they are a plant of my own, the work of my hands, wherein I may glory."[2]

The sages taught [also the following] in the style of the Mishnah; blessed be he who was pleased with them and their teaching.

1.   Rabbi Meir said: Whoever occupies himself with the study of the Torah for its own sake merits many things; nay more, the whole world is worthwhile for his sake. He is called friend, beloved; he loves God and he loves mankind; he pleases God and he pleases mankind. The Torah invests him with humility and reverence; it enables him to become righteous, godly, upright and faithful; it keeps him far from sin, and draws him near to virtue. Men are benefited by him with counsel and sound wisdom, understanding and strength, as it is said: "Mine are counsel and sound wisdom; mine are reason and might."[3] It gives him rule and dominion [personality that commands obedience] and judging ability. To him

---

לפום צערא אגרא and the preceding paragraph are given in Aramaic. In *Avoth d'Rabbi Nathan* 12:11 both sayings are ascribed to Hillel.

שנו חכמים is the Hebrew equivalent of the Aramaic תנו רבנן, used in the Talmud to introduce a *Baraitha*, a tannaitic teaching next in authority to the Mishnah. This chapter, which contains sayings of the Tannaim not included in the Mishnah, is known as *Kinyan Torah* because its subject–matter is in praise of the Torah. It is also known as *Baraitha d'Rabbi Meir* because it opens with the saying of Rabbi Meir.

---

[1] *Isaiah* 42:21.   [2] *Isaiah* 60:21.   [3] *Proverbs* 8:14.

תוֹרָה, וְנַעֲשֶׂה כְּמַעֲיָן הַמִּתְגַּבֵּר וּכְנָהָר שֶׁאֵינוֹ פוֹסֵק. וְהֹוֶה
צָנוּעַ וְאֶרֶךְ רוּחַ, וּמוֹחֵל עַל עֶלְבּוֹנוֹ. וּמְגַדַּלְתּוֹ וּמְרוֹמַמְתּוֹ עַל
כָּל הַמַּעֲשִׂים.

ב. אָמַר רַבִּי יְהוֹשֻׁעַ בֶּן לֵוִי: בְּכָל יוֹם וָיוֹם בַּת קוֹל יוֹצֵאת
מֵהַר חוֹרֵב וּמַכְרֶזֶת וְאוֹמֶרֶת: אוֹי לָהֶם לַבְּרִיּוֹת מֵעֶלְבּוֹנָהּ שֶׁל
תּוֹרָה, שֶׁכָּל מִי שֶׁאֵינוֹ עוֹסֵק בַּתּוֹרָה נִקְרָא נָזוּף, שֶׁנֶּאֱמַר: נֶזֶם
זָהָב בְּאַף חֲזִיר, אִשָּׁה יָפָה וְסָרַת טָעַם. וְאוֹמֵר: וְהַלֻּחֹת מַעֲשֵׂה
אֱלֹהִים הֵמָּה, וְהַמִּכְתָּב מִכְתַּב אֱלֹהִים הוּא, חָרוּת עַל הַלֻּחֹת.
אַל תִּקְרָא חָרוּת אֶלָּא חֵרוּת, שֶׁאֵין לְךָ בֶּן־חוֹרִין אֶלָּא מִי
שֶׁעוֹסֵק בְּתַלְמוּד תּוֹרָה; וְכָל מִי שֶׁעוֹסֵק בְּתַלְמוּד תּוֹרָה הֲרֵי
זֶה מִתְעַלֶּה, שֶׁנֶּאֱמַר: וּמִמַּתָּנָה נַחֲלִיאֵל, וּמִנַּחֲלִיאֵל בָּמוֹת.

ג. הַלּוֹמֵד מֵחֲבֵרוֹ פֶּרֶק אֶחָד, אוֹ הֲלָכָה אֶחָת, אוֹ פָּסוּק
אֶחָד, אוֹ דִּבּוּר אֶחָד, אוֹ אֲפִילוּ אוֹת אֶחָת, צָרִיךְ לִנְהָג־בּוֹ
כָּבוֹד; שֶׁכֵּן מָצִינוּ בְּדָוִד מֶלֶךְ יִשְׂרָאֵל, שֶׁלֹּא לָמַד מֵאֲחִיתֹפֶל
אֶלָּא שְׁנֵי דְבָרִים בִּלְבָד, קְרָאוֹ רַבּוֹ, אַלּוּפוֹ וּמְיֻדָּעוֹ, שֶׁנֶּאֱמַר:
וְאַתָּה אֱנוֹשׁ כְּעֶרְכִּי, אַלּוּפִי וּמְיֻדָּעִי. וַהֲלֹא דְבָרִים קַל וָחֹמֶר:
וּמַה דָּוִד מֶלֶךְ יִשְׂרָאֵל שֶׁלֹּא לָמַד מֵאֲחִיתֹפֶל אֶלָּא שְׁנֵי דְבָרִים

רבי יהושע בן לוי was one of the first generation of the *Amoraim*, whose
discussions of the mishnaic law are recorded in the Palestinian and Babylonian
Talmuds. He lived in Palestine during the middle of the third century and
became the subject of many legends.

נום זהב באף is interpreted by means of **נוטריקון** ("shorthand"). The initial
letters of **נום זהב** are combined with the last letter of **באף** to form **נוף**.

אשה יפה..., "a fair woman lacking in taste," refers here to one who has the
aptitude for Torah and makes no use of it.

אל תקרא introduces a play on words, and not an emendation of the text.

ממתנה נחליאל... The Hebrew place-names are here interpreted as if they
were common nouns.

the secrets of the Torah are revealed; he is made like a fountain, that ever gathers force, and like a never-failing stream. He becomes modest, patient, and forgiving of insults. The Torah makes him great and raises him above all creatures.

2.   Rabbi Joshua ben Levi said: Every day a heavenly voice resounds from Mount Horeb, proclaiming these words: "Woe to the people for their disregard of the Torah!" For whoever does not occupy himself with the Torah is considered rebuked, as it is said: "Like a golden ring in the snout of a swine is a fair woman lacking in taste:"[1] The Torah says: "The tablets were the work of God, and the writing was the writing of God, engraved upon the tablets."[2] Read not here *haruth* [meaning 'engraved'] but *heruth* [which means 'freedom'], for none can be considered free except those who occupy themselves with the study of the Torah. Anyone who occupies himself with the study of the Torah shall be exalted, as it is said: "Through the [Torah] gift one attains the heritage of God; by the heritage of God [one is raised] to high places."[3]

3.   He who learns from his fellow man a single section, a single rule, a single verse, a single expression, or even a single letter, ought to treat him with respect; for so we find with David, king of Israel, who learnt only two things from Ahitophel, and yet regarded him as his master, guide and intimate friend, as it is said: "You were my equal, my teacher and intimate friend."[4] This certainly presents an argument from minor to major: if David, king of Israel, who learnt only two things from Ahitophel, regarded him as his

---

הלכה a traditional opinion, a legal decision. פסוק a biblical passage. דבור a divine utterance, a biblical expression. אות refers to the correct spelling of words, whether to use א or ע for example (Kallah, chapter 8).

אחיתפל, who participated in Absalom's rebellion against David, was at first David's best friend. His wisdom was believed to be superhuman.

שני דברים בלבד two lessons only which were, according to a talmudic statement, to the effect that one should study in the company of a colleague and that it is proper to walk to the house of prayer eagerly and not leisurely (Kallah, chapter 8). It has been suggested that instead of שני דברים בלבד we should read שֶׁנִּדְבָּרִים בִּלְבָד, "who merely conversed."

---

[1] *Proverbs* 11:22.   [2] *Exodus* 32:16.   [3] *Numbers* 21:19.   [4] *Psalm* 55:14.

בְּלִבָּד, קְרָאוֹ רַבּוֹ, אַלּוּפוֹ וּמְיֻדָּעוֹ, הַלּוֹמֵד מֵחֲבֵרוֹ פֶּרֶק אֶחָד,
אוֹ הֲלָכָה אַחַת, אוֹ פָּסוּק אֶחָד, אוֹ דִבּוּר אֶחָד, אוֹ אֲפִלּוּ אוֹת
אַחַת, עַל אַחַת כַּמָּה וְכַמָּה שֶׁצָּרִיךְ לִנְהָג־בּוֹ כָּבוֹד. וְאֵין כָּבוֹד
אֶלָּא תוֹרָה, שֶׁנֶּאֱמַר: כָּבוֹד חֲכָמִים יִנְחָלוּ, וּתְמִימִים יִנְחֲלוּ
טוֹב. וְאֵין טוֹב אֶלָּא תוֹרָה, שֶׁנֶּאֱמַר: כִּי לֶקַח טוֹב נָתַתִּי לָכֶם,
תּוֹרָתִי אַל תַּעֲזֹבוּ.

ד. כָּךְ הִיא דַרְכָּהּ שֶׁל תּוֹרָה: פַּת בְּמֶלַח תֹּאכֵל, וּמַיִם
בִּמְשׂוּרָה תִשְׁתֶּה, וְעַל הָאָרֶץ תִּישָׁן, וְחַיֵּי צַעַר תִּחְיֶה, וּבַתּוֹרָה
אַתָּה עָמֵל. אִם אַתָּה עוֹשֶׂה כֵן, אַשְׁרֶיךָ וְטוֹב לָךְ; אַשְׁרֶיךָ
בָּעוֹלָם הַזֶּה, וְטוֹב לָךְ לָעוֹלָם הַבָּא.

ה. אַל תְּבַקֵּשׁ גְּדֻלָּה לְעַצְמֶךָ, וְאַל תַּחְמֹד כָּבוֹד. יוֹתֵר
מִלִּמּוּדְךָ עֲשֵׂה, וְאַל תִּתְאַוֶּה לְשֻׁלְחָנָם שֶׁל מְלָכִים, שֶׁשֻּׁלְחָנְךָ
גָּדוֹל מִשֻּׁלְחָנָם, וְכִתְרְךָ גָּדוֹל מִכִּתְרָם; וְנֶאֱמָן הוּא בַּעַל
מְלַאכְתְּךָ, שֶׁיְּשַׁלֶּם־לָךְ שְׂכַר פְּעֻלָּתֶךָ.

ו. גְּדוֹלָה תוֹרָה יוֹתֵר מִן הַכְּהֻנָּה וּמִן הַמַּלְכוּת. שֶׁהַמַּלְכוּת
נִקְנֵית בִּשְׁלֹשִׁים מַעֲלוֹת, וְהַכְּהֻנָּה נִקְנֵית בְּעֶשְׂרִים וְאַרְבַּע,
וְהַתּוֹרָה נִקְנֵית בְּאַרְבָּעִים וּשְׁמוֹנָה דְבָרִים, וְאֵלּוּ הֵן: בְּתַלְמוּד,
בִּשְׁמִיעַת הָאֹזֶן, בַּעֲרִיכַת שְׂפָתַיִם, בְּבִינַת הַלֵּב, בְּאֵימָה,
בְּיִרְאָה, בַּעֲנָוָה, בְּשִׂמְחָה, בְּטָהֳרָה, בְּשִׁמּוּשׁ חֲכָמִים, בְּדִבּוּק
חֲבֵרִים, בְּפִלְפּוּל הַתַּלְמִידִים, בְּיִשּׁוּב בְּמִקְרָא וּבְמִשְׁנָה,
בְּמִעוּט סְחוֹרָה, בְּמִעוּט דֶּרֶךְ אֶרֶץ, בְּמִעוּט תַּעֲנוּג, בְּמִעוּט
שֵׁנָה, בְּמִעוּט שִׂיחָה, בְּמִעוּט שְׂחוֹק, בְּאֹרֶךְ אַפַּיִם, בְּלֵב
טוֹב, בֶּאֱמוּנַת חֲכָמִים, בְּקַבָּלַת הַיִּסּוּרִים; הַמַּכִּיר אֶת מְקוֹמוֹ,
וְהַשָּׂמֵחַ בְּחֶלְקוֹ, וְהָעוֹשֶׂה סְיָג לִדְבָרָיו, וְאֵינוֹ מַחֲזִיק טוֹבָה
לְעַצְמוֹ, אָהוּב, אוֹהֵב אֶת הַמָּקוֹם, אוֹהֵב אֶת הַבְּרִיּוֹת, אוֹהֵב

master, guide and intimate friend, how much more ought one who
learns from his companion a section, rule, verse, expression, or
even a single letter, to treat him with respect. *Honor* implies
Torah, as it is said: "The wise shall inherit honor; men of integrity
shall attain good fortune."[1] *Good* implies Torah, as it is said:
"I give you good doctrine; forsake not my Torah."[2]

4. This is the way of Torah study: eat bread with salt, drink
water by measure, sleep on the bare ground, and live a life of hard-
ship while you toil in the Torah [study of the Torah is expected
even if one is extremely poor]. If you do this, "happy shall you be
and it shall be well with you";[3] *happy shall you be* in this world,
and it shall be well with you in the world to come.

5. Do not seek greatness for yourself and do not crave honor;
let your deeds exceed your learning; do not desire the table of kings,
for your table is greater than theirs, your crown is more glorious
than theirs; your Employer can be trusted to pay you for your
work.

6. The Torah is greater than priesthood or royalty; for royalty
is acquired by virtue of thirty qualifications, and priesthood by
twenty-four, while the Torah is acquired by forty-eight, namely:
study, attentive listening, ordered speech [audible rehearsing],
mental alertness, awe [in the student's attitude towards his mas-
ter], reverence [for God], humility, cheerfulness, ethical purity,
attendance on scholars, close association with colleagues, discussion with students, sedateness, knowledge of Scriptures and
Mishnah, moderation in business, moderation in worldly interests,
moderation in pleasure, moderation in sleep, moderation in conversation, moderation in merriment, patience, a good heart [un-
selfishness], intellectual honesty, uncomplaining acceptance of
chastisement, knowing one's place, being content with one's lot,
setting a limit to one's words, claiming no credit for oneself, being
beloved, loving God, loving mankind, loving righteousness, loving

---

[1] *Proverbs* 3:35;28:10.   [2] *Proverbs* 4:2.   [3] *Psalm* 128:2.

אֶת הַצְּדָקוֹת, אוֹהֵב אֶת הַמֵּישָׁרִים, אוֹהֵב אֶת הַתּוֹכָחוֹת,
וּמִתְרַחֵק מִן הַכָּבוֹד, וְלֹא מֵגִיס לִבּוֹ בְּתַלְמוּדוֹ, וְאֵינוֹ שָׂמֵחַ
בְּהוֹרָאָה, נוֹשֵׂא בְעֹל עִם חֲבֵרוֹ, וּמַכְרִיעוֹ לְכַף זְכוּת, וּמַעֲמִידוֹ
עַל הָאֱמֶת, וּמַעֲמִידוֹ עַל הַשָּׁלוֹם, וּמִתְיַשֵּׁב בְּתַלְמוּדוֹ, שׁוֹאֵל
וּמֵשִׁיב, שׁוֹמֵעַ וּמוֹסִיף, הַלּוֹמֵד עַל מְנָת לְלַמֵּד, וְהַלּוֹמֵד עַל
מְנָת לַעֲשׂוֹת, הַמַּחְכִּים אֶת רַבּוֹ, וְהַמְכַוֵּן אֶת שְׁמוּעָתוֹ, וְהָאוֹמֵר
דָּבָר בְּשֵׁם אוֹמְרוֹ. הָא לָמַדְתָּ, כָּל הָאוֹמֵר דָּבָר בְּשֵׁם אוֹמְרוֹ,
מֵבִיא גְאֻלָּה לָעוֹלָם, שֶׁנֶּאֱמַר: וַתֹּאמֶר אֶסְתֵּר לַמֶּלֶךְ בְּשֵׁם
מָרְדְּכָי.

ז. גְּדוֹלָה תוֹרָה שֶׁהִיא נוֹתֶנֶת חַיִּים לְעוֹשֶׂיהָ בָּעוֹלָם הַזֶּה
וּבָעוֹלָם הַבָּא, שֶׁנֶּאֱמַר: כִּי חַיִּים הֵם לְמֹצְאֵיהֶם, וּלְכָל בְּשָׂרוֹ
מַרְפֵּא. וְאוֹמֵר: רִפְאוּת תְּהִי לְשָׁרֶּךָ, וְשִׁקּוּי לְעַצְמוֹתֶיךָ.
וְאוֹמֵר: עֵץ חַיִּים הִיא לַמַּחֲזִיקִים בָּהּ, וְתֹמְכֶיהָ מְאֻשָּׁר. וְאוֹמֵר:
כִּי לִוְיַת חֵן הֵם לְרֹאשֶׁךָ, וַעֲנָקִים לְגַרְגְּרֹתֶיךָ. וְאוֹמֵר: תִּתֵּן
לְרֹאשְׁךָ לִוְיַת חֵן, עֲטֶרֶת תִּפְאֶרֶת תְּמַגְּנֶךָ. וְאוֹמֵר: כִּי בִי יִרְבּוּ
יָמֶיךָ, וְיוֹסִיפוּ לְךָ שְׁנוֹת חַיִּים. וְאוֹמֵר: אֹרֶךְ יָמִים בִּימִינָהּ,
בִּשְׂמֹאולָהּ עֹשֶׁר וְכָבוֹד. וְאוֹמֵר: כִּי אֹרֶךְ יָמִים וּשְׁנוֹת חַיִּים
וְשָׁלוֹם יוֹסִיפוּ לָךְ. וְאוֹמֵר: דְּרָכֶיהָ דַרְכֵי נֹעַם, וְכָל נְתִיבוֹתֶיהָ
שָׁלוֹם.

ח. רַבִּי שִׁמְעוֹן בֶּן יְהוּדָה, מִשּׁוּם רַבִּי שִׁמְעוֹן בֶּן יוֹחַאי, אוֹמֵר:
הַנּוֹי, וְהַכֹּחַ, וְהָעֹשֶׁר, וְהַכָּבוֹד, וְהַחָכְמָה, הַזִּקְנָה וְהַשֵּׂיבָה,
וְהַבָּנִים, נָאֶה לַצַּדִּיקִים וְנָאֶה לָעוֹלָם, שֶׁנֶּאֱמַר: עֲטֶרֶת תִּפְאֶרֶת
שֵׂיבָה, בְּדֶרֶךְ צְדָקָה תִּמָּצֵא. וְאוֹמֵר: תִּפְאֶרֶת בַּחוּרִים כֹּחָם,

רבי שמעון בן יהודה belonged to the fourth generation of the *Tannaim* and lived towards the end of the second century.

equity, loving reproof, shunning honors, taking no pride in one's learning, not delighting in dictating decisions, bearing the yoke with one's colleague, judging him favorably, directing him to truth and peace, being composed in one's study, asking and answering, listening and adding to one's knowledge, learning in order to teach, learning in order to practise, making his teacher wiser, noting with precision what one has learnt, and reporting a thing in the name of the person who said it. You may infer that whoever reports a thing in the name of the person who said it brings deliverance into the world, for it is said: "And Esther told the king in the name of Mordecai."[1]

7.   Great is Torah, for it gives to those who fulfill it life in this world and in the world to come, as it is said: "For they are life to those who find them, health to all their flesh." "It shall be health to your body, marrow to your bones." "It is a tree of life to those who take hold of it; happy are those who support it." "They shall be a graceful garland for your head, a necklace around your neck." "It shall place on your head a graceful garland; a crown of glory shall it bestow on you." "By me your days shall be multiplied, the years of your life shall be increased." "Long life is in its right hand; in its left hand are riches and honor." "Length of days, years of life and peace, shall they add to you." "Its ways are ways of pleasantness, and all its paths are peace."[2]

8.   Rabbi Simeon ben Judah said in the name of Rabbi Simeon ben Yoḥai: Beauty and strength, wealth and honor, wisdom and age, gray hair and children are comely to the righteous and comely to the world, as it is said: "Gray hair is a crown of glory, to be found in the path of righteousness." "The glory of the young

רבי שמעון בן יוחאי was one of the most brilliant disciples of Rabbi Akiba. A large number of students attended his lectures in Galilee. The Romans condemned him to death because he was accusing them of selfishness and immorality. He fled together with his son Rabbi Elazar and took refuge in a cave for thirteen years. His fame as a mystic became so great that the kabbalistic work *Zohar* has been attributed to him.

הנוי והכח והעשר are obviously good things and do not seem to require proof to that effect. It has therefore been suggested that the biblical texts are quoted here chiefly on behalf of old age and children, because these do not appear to be unmixed blessings.

---

[1] *Esther* 2:22.   [2] *Proverbs* 4:22; 3:8; 3:18; 1:9; 4:9; 9:11; 3:16; 3:2, 17.

וַהֲדַר זְקֵנִים שֵׁיבָה. וְאוֹמֵר: עֲטֶרֶת חֲכָמִים עָשְׁרָם. וְאוֹמֵר: עֲטֶרֶת זְקֵנִים בְּנֵי בָנִים, וְתִפְאֶרֶת בָּנִים אֲבוֹתָם. וְאוֹמֵר: וְחָפְרָה הַלְּבָנָה וּבוֹשָׁה הַחַמָּה, כִּי מָלַךְ יְיָ צְבָאוֹת בְּהַר צִיּוֹן וּבִירוּשָׁלַיִם, וְנֶגֶד זְקֵנָיו כָּבוֹד. רַבִּי שִׁמְעוֹן בֶּן מְנַסְיָא אוֹמֵר: אֵלּוּ שֶׁבַע מִדּוֹת שֶׁמָּנוּ חֲכָמִים לַצַּדִּיקִים, כֻּלָּם נִתְקַיְּמוּ בְּרַבִּי וּבְבָנָיו.

ט. אָמַר רַבִּי יוֹסֵי בֶּן קִסְמָא: פַּעַם אַחַת הָיִיתִי מְהַלֵּךְ בַּדֶּרֶךְ, וּפָגַע בִּי אָדָם אֶחָד וְנָתַן לִי שָׁלוֹם, וְהֶחֱזַרְתִּי לוֹ שָׁלוֹם. אָמַר לִי: רַבִּי, מֵאֵיזֶה מָקוֹם אָתָּה. אָמַרְתִּי לוֹ: מֵעִיר גְּדוֹלָה שֶׁל חֲכָמִים וְשֶׁל סוֹפְרִים אֲנִי. אָמַר לִי: רַבִּי, רְצוֹנְךָ שֶׁתָּדוּר עִמָּנוּ בִּמְקוֹמֵנוּ, וַאֲנִי אֶתֵּן לְךָ אֶלֶף אַלְפִים דִּינְרֵי זָהָב וַאֲבָנִים טוֹבוֹת וּמַרְגָּלִיּוֹת. אָמַרְתִּי לוֹ: אִם אַתָּה נוֹתֵן לִי כָּל כֶּסֶף וְזָהָב וַאֲבָנִים טוֹבוֹת וּמַרְגָּלִיּוֹת שֶׁבָּעוֹלָם, אֵינִי דָר אֶלָּא בִּמְקוֹם תּוֹרָה. וְכֵן כָּתוּב בְּסֵפֶר תְּהִלִּים עַל יְדֵי דָוִד מֶלֶךְ יִשְׂרָאֵל: טוֹב לִי תוֹרַת פִּיךָ מֵאַלְפֵי זָהָב וָכָסֶף. וְלֹא עוֹד, אֶלָּא שֶׁבִּשְׁעַת פְּטִירָתוֹ שֶׁל אָדָם אֵין מְלַוִּים לוֹ לְאָדָם לֹא כֶּסֶף, וְלֹא זָהָב, וְלֹא אֲבָנִים טוֹבוֹת וּמַרְגָּלִיּוֹת, אֶלָּא תוֹרָה וּמַעֲשִׂים טוֹבִים בִּלְבָד, שֶׁנֶּאֱמַר: בְּהִתְהַלֶּכְךָ תַּנְחֶה אֹתָךְ, בְּשָׁכְבְּךָ תִּשְׁמֹר עָלֶיךָ, וַהֲקִיצוֹתָ הִיא תְשִׂיחֶךָ. בְּהִתְהַלֶּכְךָ תַּנְחֶה אֹתָךְ, בָּעוֹלָם הַזֶּה; בְּשָׁכְבְּךָ תִּשְׁמֹר עָלֶיךָ, בַּקֶּבֶר; וַהֲקִיצוֹתָ הִיא תְשִׂיחֶךָ, לָעוֹלָם הַבָּא. וְאוֹמֵר: לִי הַכֶּסֶף וְלִי הַזָּהָב, נְאֻם יְיָ צְבָאוֹת.

י. חֲמִשָּׁה קִנְיָנִים קָנָה הַקָּדוֹשׁ בָּרוּךְ הוּא בְּעוֹלָמוֹ. וְאֵלּוּ הֵן: תּוֹרָה קִנְיָן אֶחָד, שָׁמַיִם וָאָרֶץ קִנְיָן אֶחָד, אַבְרָהָם קִנְיָן אֶחָד, יִשְׂרָאֵל קִנְיָן אֶחָד, בֵּית הַמִּקְדָּשׁ קִנְיָן אֶחָד. תּוֹרָה מִנַּיִן,

---

רבי שמעון בן מנסיא was a contemporary of Rabbi Judah ha-Nasi.
רבי יוסי בן קסמא lived at the beginning of the second century.

men is their strength, and the beauty of old men is gray hair."
"The crown of the wise is their riches." "Grandchildren are the
crown of old men, and fathers are the pride of their children."[1]
And it says: "The moon shall be confounded and the sun ashamed;
for the Lord of hosts will be King on Mount Zion and in Jerusalem,
and there shall be glory before the elders of his people."[2]

Rabbi Simeon ben Menasya said: These seven qualities, which
the sages have enumerated as becoming to the righteous, were all
realized in Rabbi Judah ha-Nasi and his sons.

9. Rabbi Yosé ben Kisma said: I was once travelling on the
road when a man met me and greeted me, and I returned his
greeting. He said to me: "Rabbi, from what place are you?" I
said to him: "I come from a great city of sages and scholars." He
said to me: "Rabbi, are you willing to live with us in our place?
I will give you a million golden dinars, and precious stones and
pearls." I told him: "Were you to give me all the silver and gold
and precious stones and pearls in the world, I would not live any-
where except in a place of Torah." In a like manner, it is written
in the Book of Psalms by David, king of Israel: "Thy own teaching
means more to me than thousands in gold and silver."[3] Further-
more, when a man dies, neither silver nor gold nor precious stones
nor pearls accompany him, but Torah and good deeds alone, as it
is said: "When you walk, it shall guide you; when you lie down,
it shall watch over you; and when you awake, it shall talk with
you."[4] *When you walk, it shall guide you* in this world; *when you lie
down, it shall watch over you* in the grave; *and when you awake, it
shall talk with you* in the world to come. It says also: "Mine is the
silver and mine is the gold, says the Lord of hosts."[5]

10. Five possessions has the Holy One, blessed be he, specifi-
cally declared his own in his world, namely: the Torah, heaven
and earth, Abraham, Israel, and the sanctuary. How do we know
this about the Torah? Because it is written: "The Lord possessed

---

[1] *Proverbs* 16:31; 20:29; 14:24; 17:6.   [2] *Isaiah* 24:23.   [3] *Psalm* 119:72.
[4] *Proverbs* 6:22.   [5] *Haggai* 2:8.

דִּכְתִיב: יְיָ קָנָנִי רֵאשִׁית דַּרְכּוֹ, קֶדֶם מִפְעָלָיו מֵאָז. שָׁמַיִם וָאָרֶץ
מִנַּיִן, דִּכְתִיב: כֹּה אָמַר יְיָ, הַשָּׁמַיִם כִּסְאִי, וְהָאָרֶץ הֲדֹם רַגְלַי,
אֵי־זֶה בַיִת אֲשֶׁר תִּבְנוּ לִי, וְאֵי־זֶה מָקוֹם מְנוּחָתִי. וְאוֹמֵר: מָה
רַבּוּ מַעֲשֶׂיךָ, יְיָ, כֻּלָּם בְּחָכְמָה עָשִׂיתָ, מָלְאָה הָאָרֶץ קִנְיָנֶךָ.
אַבְרָהָם מִנַּיִן, דִּכְתִיב: וַיְבָרְכֵהוּ וַיֹּאמַר, בָּרוּךְ אַבְרָם לְאֵל
עֶלְיוֹן, קֹנֵה שָׁמַיִם וָאָרֶץ. יִשְׂרָאֵל מִנַּיִן, דִּכְתִיב: עַד יַעֲבֹר
עַמְּךָ, יְיָ, עַד יַעֲבֹר עַם זוּ קָנִיתָ; וְאוֹמֵר: לִקְדוֹשִׁים אֲשֶׁר בָּאָרֶץ
הֵמָּה, וְאַדִּירֵי כָּל חֶפְצִי בָם. בֵּית הַמִּקְדָּשׁ מִנַּיִן, דִּכְתִיב: מָכוֹן
לְשִׁבְתְּךָ פָּעַלְתָּ, יְיָ, מִקְּדָשׁ, אֲדֹנָי, כּוֹנְנוּ יָדֶיךָ; וְאוֹמֵר: וַיְבִיאֵם
אֶל גְּבוּל קָדְשׁוֹ, הַר זֶה קָנְתָה יְמִינוֹ.

יא. כֹּל מַה שֶּׁבָּרָא הַקָּדוֹשׁ בָּרוּךְ הוּא בְּעוֹלָמוֹ, לֹא בְרָאוֹ
אֶלָּא לִכְבוֹדוֹ, שֶׁנֶּאֱמַר: כֹּל הַנִּקְרָא בִשְׁמִי, וְלִכְבוֹדִי בְּרָאתִיו,
יְצַרְתִּיו אַף עֲשִׂיתִיו. וְאוֹמֵר: יְיָ יִמְלֹךְ לְעֹלָם וָעֶד.

רַבִּי חֲנַנְיָא בֶּן עֲקַשְׁיָא אוֹמֵר: רָצָה הַקָּדוֹשׁ בָּרוּךְ הוּא
לְזַכּוֹת אֶת יִשְׂרָאֵל, לְפִיכָךְ הִרְבָּה לָהֶם תּוֹרָה וּמִצְוֹת, שֶׁנֶּאֱמַר:
יְיָ חָפֵץ לְמַעַן צִדְקוֹ, יַגְדִּיל תּוֹרָה וְיַאְדִּיר.

אברהם is entirely omitted in parallel passages enumerating these special
possessions. The biblical text, קונה שמים וארץ, refers directly to heaven and
earth as the possession of God, and does not seem to support the idea that
Abraham was called *kinyan*. According to the opinion of Rabbi Elijah, the
Wilna Gaon, this passage should be emended to include four possessions
instead of five.

קדושים is taken here to refer to Israel as the people sanctified by God's
commandments.

כל מה שברא amplifies the thought expressed in the preceding paragraph.
The whole creation bears witness that everything has come into being for a
noble and lofty purpose.

רבי חנניא בן עקשיא lived during the second century of the common era.
This paragraph, found at the close of the tractate Makkoth, is repeated at the
end of each of the six chapters of *Avoth* in order to emphasize the thought that

me first of his creation, first of all his works in days of old."[1] How do we know this about heaven and earth? Because it is written: "Thus says the Lord: The heaven is my throne, and the earth is my footstool; what manner of house would you build for me, what manner of place as my residence?"[2] It says also: "How manifold are thy works, O Lord! In wisdom hast thou made them all; the earth is full of thy possessions."[3] How do we know this about Abraham? Because it is written: "And he blessed him and said: Blessed be Abram of God Most High, Possessor of heaven and earth."[4] How do we know this about Israel? Because it is written: "Until thy people pass over, O Lord; until the people whom thou possessest pass over."[5] It says also: "As for the holy people who are on earth, they are the nobles in whom is all my delight."[6] How do we know this about the sanctuary? Because it is written: "The place of thy abode which thou, O Lord, hast made; the sanctuary, O Lord, which thy hands have established."[7] It says also: "And he brought them to the region of his sanctuary, to the mountain which his might had acquired."[8]

11. Whatever the Holy One, blessed be he, created in his world, he created only for his glory, as it is said: "Everything that is called by my name, it is for my glory that I have created it; I have formed it, I have made it."[9] It says also: "The Lord shall reign forever and ever."[10]

Rabbi Ḥananyah ben Akashyah said: The Holy One, blessed be he, desired to purify Israel; hence he gave them a Torah rich in rules of conduct, as it is said: "The Lord was pleased, for the sake of [Israel's] righteousness, to render the Torah great and glorious."[11]

---

the Torah was given as a mark of divine love and was designed to train Israel in holiness.

לזכות את ישראל to cause Israel to be צדיקים=זכאים ("righteous"). The Targum renders צדיק by זכאי (Genesis 6:9). למען צדקו is here used homiletically in the sense that God meant to make Israel righteous, though literally the phrase refers to God's own righteousness.

---

[1]*Proverbs* 8:22. [2]*Isaiah* 66:1. [3]*Psalm* 104:24. [4]*Genesis* 14:19. [5]*Exodus* 15:16. [6]*Psalm* 16:3. [7]*Exodus* 15:17. [8]*Psalm* 78:54. [9]*Isaiah* 43:7. [10]*Exodus* 15:18. [11]*Isaiah* 42:21.

Printed in the United States
98013LV00011B/335/A

9 781432 596439